AUDACIOUS VOICES

AUDACIOUS VOICES

PROFILES IN INTERSECTIONAL FEMINISM

Holly J. Blake
and Melissa D. Ooten

SHE WRITES PRESS

Published November 13, 2018
Printed in the United States of America
Print ISBN: 978-1-63152-491-2
E-ISBN: 978-1-63152-492-9
Library of Congress Control Number: 2018947565

For information, address:
She Writes Press
1563 Solano Ave #546
Berkeley, CA 94707

Interior design by Tabitha Lahr

She Writes Press is a division of SparkPoint Studio, LLC.

Names and identifying characteristics have been changed to protect the privacy of certain individuals.

CONTENTS

FOREWORD
by Courtney E. Martin

In the inaugural issue of *Ms. Magazine* in December of 1971, Jane O'Reilly wrote a description of a consciousness raising group—women sitting in a circle, sharing the stories of their lives, and realizing that they were linked by an invisible thread of misogony: "they will recognize the click! of recognition, that parenthesis of truth around a little thing that completes the puzzle of reality in women's minds—the moment that brings a gleam to our eyes and means the revolution has begun."

The click moment, as it has come to be known, was born.

I wasn't yet born when Jane wrote those fateful words. In fact, my mom could very well have been one of those women sitting on the living room rug of a friend, locating her outrage for the first time. She was an undergrad at Colorado State University at the time, part of the Civil Rights protests there and very much discovering her own ambitions beyond the prescribed gender scripts of the time. She didn't have any women's studies classes, but she found her "professors" in books. In 1983, when the *Women's Review of Books* was first published, she subscribed immediately. That and *Ms. Magazine* would show up consistently on our kitchen table as I was growing up. Feminism was in the water.

And yet, I still needed my own click moment to fully embrace my feminist identity. As an undergrad at Barnard College, I saw Amy Richards and Jennifer Baumgardner speak and—just like Jane wrote—click! If they were feminists, then I wanted to be one, too. I devoured their book, *Manifesta*, while studying abroad in Cape Town, South Africa, and studying the fall of apartheid. I was just starting to put the intersectional pieces together—how sexism intertwined with racism intertwined with classism, etc. There is not, as it turns out, an invisible thread of misogony alone, but a tangled knot of so many forms of interpersonal and structural inequity.

But here's the thing about consciousness. It doesn't actually work like a light switch. Once you turn it on, you can't turn it back off. And turning it on is just the first tiny step, however significant it might feel. The ways in which your consciousness continues to evolve and how you actually apply what you realize in the beautiful, horrible world—that's the really juicy story.

As it turns out, that's the story sitting in your hot little hands. Or more accurately, the stories. Twelve people, whose click moments largely took place in the context of one remarkable program, and the struggle and triumph that came after.

It's such a special book for a couple of reasons. First of all, while those of us who have been lucky enough to take women, gender, and sexuality studies (WGSS) classes, or have amazing feminists teach classes outside of WGSS departments but with the same principles, know—being (re)educated in this way is a huge personal and political gift. WGSS classrooms are where some of the most radical, interesting work in consciousness raising is happening today. Sure, a lot of that is also happening online and through TED talks and Janelle Monáe videos and between friends and in the pages of great contemporary feminist thinkers. But there is still nothing that replaces a group of people sitting around a table, hashing out the injustices and opportunities for healing in the world, and in our lives, with a great teacher. This book names that and makes it come to life. For those who teach, it will be a great inspiration for how to produce more, and more durable, click moments.

But the other reason this book is so special is that it doesn't leave the click in the classroom. It follows these amazing humans as they try to apply what they've learned long after they've walked across the graduation stage. How do we actually use our own shifts in consciousness to change workplaces, policies, even our own families? How do we maintain our sense of solidarity when our fellow students aren't sitting beside us? How do we weather the inevitable failure of intersectional activism in an unfinished revolution?

These are questions each person has to live into for themselves, but these twelve authors are great models for asking courageously. Readers will gain strength from them, appreciate their humility, and get ideas about how to actually shift power. They will know that they are not alone in their own journey of translating what happens inside of their heads and hearts to everyday action that can change communities and nations.

The point is not the click; it's the long tail of consciousness and what we do with it. Just as the point is not to land on an answer, some perfect way of translating feminism into the world, but to keep asking and pursuing the questions. This is our responsibility and gift, as these twelve authors point out so eloquently and variably. The gleam is still alight. The revolution continues.

ACKNOWLEDGMENTS

The impetus for this book emerged from our deeply held belief that a critical feminist education that combines theoretical knowledge with practical application can transform lives. The WILL* program fully embodies this type of education, and we both feel extremely grateful to have made administering the program our professional work for many years now. The holistic nature of WILL* allows us to engage in meaningful ways with a wide range of thoughtful, passionate students who truly care about the world, their place in it, and how to make it a better, more equitable place for everyone to live. The best feminist work is collaborative, and the WILL* program would not be the success it is without the guidance and knowledge our students bring to it, and to us, day in and day out.

We have many people to thank for both participating in and supporting the work of the WILL* program. One of the strengths of the program is its vibrancy; it's never static. It not only changes as the academic field of women, gender, and sexuality studies (WGSS) changes, but it also evolves in response to student ideas and initiatives. Therefore, first and foremost, we want to thank all of the students and graduates of the program. Without their passion for this work, the program would not have flourished and been the success that it is. We are deeply indebted to every one of our current and former students for their engagement and manifold contributions to the program, which will celebrate its fortieth anniversary in 2020.

We next want to thank the many alums who participated in the lengthy process of bookmaking with us. We began by interviewing twenty-four people and had to painstakingly narrow that group to the twelve who we worked with to create the final project. Our deepest gratitude and thanks go to these alums for their patience and commitment to the project over the years. For taking the time to be interviewed and helping us build a strong foundation for this project, we would like to thank:

Elena Adamo
Geeta Bhagchandani
Ellen Bradley
Shelley Francis
Amy Hover
Pamela Johnson Branch
Farheen Khurrum
Elizabeth MacKenzie Biedell
Allison Marsh Bogdanovic
Sarah Singletary
Kristen Tilley
Juletta Tyson

We also want to recognize our twelve contributors, who have endured several major shifts in the project and many back-and-forth conversations as we have collectively brought this book to fruition. This collection would never have emerged if they had not been as committed to the project as we were. You will meet them in the pages to follow, but we want to thank and introduce them by name here:

Jah Akande
Sharvari Dalal-Dheini
Emmanuella Delva

ACKNOWLEDGMENTS

Cammie Dunaway
Jill Eisenberg
Lisa Gray
Laura Haddad
Camille Hammond
Emily Miller
Mary Mittell
Allison Speicher
Jennifer Stolarski

We also want to thank those faculty, staff, and graduates of the University of Richmond who have served as members of the WILL* advisory board over the years. Their feedback and guidance have been crucial to the growth and strength of the program. In addition, WILL* has benefitted from the sustained support of the University of Richmond; in particular, we would like to thank Steve Bisese, Vice President for Student Development. Another special thank you goes to the Robins Foundation, whose grant in the 1990s enabled the program to expand and deepen its work.

WILL* and WGSS have a strong and mutually support-ive relationship, as WGSS serves as the academic foundation of the WILL* program. It has been rewarding and energizing work to collaborate with the WGSS program and its faculty over the years.

WILL* is strategically situated within Westhampton College at the University of Richmond. Founded in 1914 to educate women six years before the ratification of the nine-teenth amendment, Westhampton continues its progressive legacy, and today welcomes women and gender expansive students. The work of the WILL* program, and specifically this project, would not have been possible without the strong support of successive deans of Westhampton College. We particularly want to thank Patricia C. Harwood, a powerful advocate of the WILL* program in the 1990s; Juliette Land-phair, under whom this book project began; and Mia Reinoso

Genoni, who has enthusiastically supported the program and this project since becoming dean in 2016.

The four founders of the WILL* program—Dean Stephanie Bennett-Smith, and Professors Kathleen Rohaly, Jane Hopkins, and William Walker—also deserve notable mention. Together, they had the vision and the commitment to create a transformative program predicated on connecting coursework in what was then women's studies to praxis. Their work, which created the program in 1980, continues to live on both in today's thriving program at Westhampton and in replicated programs at various other colleges and universities around the country.

Courtney Martin, author, activist, and friend, has been supportive of this project from the beginning. We met in 2007 when she spoke about her first book, *Perfect Girls, Starving Daughters: How the Quest for Perfection is Harming Young Women*, at the University of Richmond. She connected powerfully with our students and with us; we have been in touch ever since. She represents the very best of feminist collaboration, generously sharing her time, extensive insight, and great passion for making this world a better, more equitable place.

Courtney Martin also introduced us to the work of She Writes Press. We are thrilled that this book is being published by She Writes Press, a publisher that intentionally centers the work and community of women writers. From copyediting to book design to publicity, it's been a truly enjoyable and rewarding collaboration.

Finally, a brief note about us. Known collectively as "the doctors" by our current students, we have shared the work of this program for many years. Holly began in 1992 and Melissa in 2005. Over that time, we have learned a great deal from one another, shared many of life's ups and downs, and finely honed our sense of humor together. We count ourselves most fortunate to be both colleagues and friends.

INTRODUCTION

Audacious.

Adjective
1. showing a willingness to take surprising or bold risks.

The word *audacious* originated in the sixteenth century, its definition rooted in concepts of boldness and daring. Its meaning evokes grit, nerve, spunk, and being gutsy. It is often defined in opposition to meekness, timidity, and fear.

Audaciousness is what this collection of stories showcases: twelve ordinary people who have had the determination and boldness to make their communities better places, who take an activist approach to living their personal and professional lives. Despite distinct backgrounds and experiences, they are all graduates of a four-year, feminist-driven university program called WILL* that challenged, informed, and strengthened their views about justice and equity, a program that motivated them to act on their values in the larger world around them.[1] We hope that these stories will encourage and inspire you; perhaps you will see some of your own experiences reflected in them.[2]

Read on if you want to learn how a diverse group of individuals continues not only to think deeply about societal problems after graduation, but also to act on that knowledge in their daily lives. Read on if you are interested in cultivating a similar educational program or curriculum to develop engaged citizens, everyday people who share an enduring commitment to making the world a better place in both unexpected and ordinary ways. Read on if you want to find inspiration to work for bettering your own communities or, for those who are already doing that work, to find solace and reassurance in the fact that many others are laboring alongside you in neighborhoods around the world.

This collection of personal narratives serves as a partial antidote to the distressing times in which we live. As we finish writing this introduction, a known misogynist and xenophobe sits in office as the forty-fifth president of the United States, having defeated Hilary Clinton, the first female major party candidate for president. Since that time, we have seen a resurgence of feminist movement-building, starting with the Women's March in January 2017 and continuing with an historic number of women elected to Virginia's legislative body in November 2017, an election considered by many to be one of the first referendums on Trump's presidency. This book captures the renewed spirit many feminists have exhibited as they have made their activist work more visible and communal. By showcasing the hope and resiliency of twelve feminists who incorporate social change work into both their professional and personal lives, this anthology offers a respite and a call to action in the midst of widespread fear-mongering and anxiety.

Trump's ascendency reflects many deep-seated and entrenched problems that were present long before November 2016. There are numerous pernicious ways in which people living in poverty and people who represent historically marginalized genders, sexualities, and races face suffocating inequity in our country. Consider these facts:

- Congressional representation by women is abysmal. Women comprise slightly less than 20 percent of the 115th Congress. While that's the highest proportion yet, it still means that in a nation that is majority female, less than one in five of our Congressional representatives are women. Nations around the world have bypassed the US on this measure. While the US ranked 52nd in terms of women's representation in government worldwide in the 1990s, it now ranks 97th.[3]

- The wage gap remains stagnant. Most women with jobs similar to men make only about 80 percent of what men make. And that gap grows when we compare women of color to white men. In the largest gap, for example, Latina workers earn only 61 percent of what white men make.[4] Beyond the basic issue of equity and fairness, income determines people's ability to support themselves and their families. Scholars have long noted the feminization of poverty worldwide: as many as 70 percent of people who reside in poverty are women and girls.

- Being a mother has become such a disadvantaged position in the workplace that sociologists have coined the term "motherhood penalty." The motherhood penalty acknowledges the systemic inequalities in pay, promotion, benefits, and perceived competence that mothers face in relation to non-mothers.[5] In terms of money, mothers lose about 5 percent of their pay per child while men often receive a fatherhood "bonus," seeing their pay boosted by 6 percent per child.[6] The United States also provides no paid parental leave for workers; it remains one of the only countries in the world not to offer paid leave to new mothers.[7] Keep in mind that 40 percent of all US households with children under the age of eighteen have mothers who are the sole or primary breadwinners, making this issue even more pressing.[8]

- Access to reproductive services is constantly under attack, both through the continual threatened defunding of Planned Parenthood and increased restrictions on abortion procedures. Access to safe abortions is much more restricted today than it was in the years following the 1973 *Roe v. Wade* decision legalizing it. And as research shows, increased restrictions don't lower the number of abortions. They simply make them more difficult and dangerous for women.[9]

- Trans women of color are being killed at an incredibly alarming rate. A report by the Inter-American Commission on Human Rights documented at least 594 LGBTQ people who were killed over a fifteen-month period across the Americas. Nearly half of those murdered were trans women of color. Because the study only included people known to be part of the LGBTQ community, those numbers are likely much higher.[10]

- The #BlackLivesMatter movement is a powerful response to entrenched anti-Black racism in our society, but its founders, Alicia Garza, Patrisse Cullors, and Opal Tometi, three queer women of color, have repeatedly noted how mainstream media has focused on the leadership of straight men within the movement. Within Black communities, Garza emphasizes, "we also want to be having the conversation about the leadership of women, and the leadership of queer folks, and the leadership of trans folks, as folks who are often left out of the narrative but who are also often doing most of the actual work."[11]

Clearly, societal problems abound. But the people in this book refuse to accept these existing conditions as the norm. Through a multiplicity of actions, they live their lives with courage and conviction, bringing about change in small and big ways, using the power of a feminist education to help them realize their visions. Their stories, told in their words, illustrate how they have taken the concepts they gained through the WILL* program and applied them in their work, in their personal relationships, and in the communities in which they live. Not surprisingly, they offer very different narratives. But what they share is a commitment to making positive social change.

An Introduction to the WILL Program*

The WILL* program was founded in 1980 at the University of Richmond, a small, liberal arts college in Virginia that graduates about eight hundred students each year.[12] WILL* is a four-year program with approximately twenty-five new students accepted annually. In addition to assorted majors, all students in WILL* graduate with a minor in women, gender, and sexuality studies (WGSS), the academic foundation of the program. WILL* takes this curricular content and amplifies it by providing students with the tools and structure they need to act on their learning.

Two guiding frameworks undergird the program's work both in and out of the classroom: intersectionality and bridging theory and praxis. Although originally focused almost exclusively on women's leadership, WILL* now emphasizes what lawyer and critical race theorist Kimberlé Crenshaw named in 1989 as "intersectionality," a concept describing how intersecting identities such as race, class, gender, and related systems of oppression and privilege inform our everyday lives.[13] For example, intersectionality makes visible how women of color experience sexism and racism, while white women experience sexism and white privilege.[14] The concept of intersectionality and the practice of employing it to better understand structural inequities deeply informs the WILL* program.

While the term "intersectionality" was newly coined in 1989, the conceptual thinking behind it has a deep history rooted in Black feminist thought reaching back to the 1800s.[15] In 1977, a collective of Black feminists known as the Combahee River Collective issued a statement in which they created "an integrated analysis and practice based upon the fact that the major systems of oppression are interlocking." The collective announced that for them, as Black lesbian women, "the synthesis of these oppressions creates the conditions of our lives."[16] In 1981, a group of radical feminist scholars of color published *This Bridge Called My Back: Writings by Radical Women of Color*, edited by Cherríe Moraga and Gloria E. Anzaldúa. This collection had far-reaching impact not only for its activist-focused framework but also for the ways in which it explicitly linked feminism, race, class, and sexuality. The writings in *This Bridge Called My Back* centered the analyses of feminists of color as well as their critiques of a mainstream feminism that too often prioritized issues that mostly affected white, middle-class women.[17] Scholars and activists including Barbara Smith, Patricia Bell Scott, Gloria Hull, bell hooks, and Patricia Hill Collins have argued for the significance of identifying multiple and interlocking systems of oppression. Their analyses marked a significant paradigm shift by centering the experiences and knowledge of the most marginalized.[18]

The second framework of the WILL* program bridges the divide between theory and praxis, meaning that it strives to link what students learn in the classroom to what happens outside of it. By praxis, we draw on the definition used by philosopher Paulo Freire that action must include critical reflection if one's work is to be transformative.[19] Coursework in WGSS helps students to think in intersectional ways about identity and power; students learn to investigate and analyze today's most pressing social justice problems from a variety of different angles. The program then provides many opportunities for them to apply what they are learning in the classroom to real-life experiences on campus and in the local Richmond community. Most recently, for example, students partnered with Advocates for Richmond Youth, an organization formed by and for youth experiencing homelessness in Richmond. Together, they turned extensive research findings into infographics to educate key stakeholders: school administrators, policy makers, community partners, service providers, and youth themselves.

Through required internships, students also connect what they learn in the classroom to the broader work of social justice. By examining their internship sites through a WGSS lens, students study organizational hierarchies to see who is in charge. For example, they ask questions about whether women hold leadership positions and how many people of color are represented. They discover whether their employers have official anti-harassment policies and who those policies do and do not cover. They ask if parental leave is offered, and if so, whether it is offered to all parents, regardless of gender. These questions help students to better understand the intricacies of workplace policies and what must be changed in order to achieve equity. Inspired in the classroom, students also pursue their own initiatives. After a lecture on the Americans with Disabilities Act one semester, a group of students met with a variety of administrators on campus to advocate for better accessibility across campus. Other initiatives have included lobbying for legislation at the Virginia General Assembly to protect LGBTQ workers in the state, mentoring in local schools, and working at local domestic violence shelters. These many opportunities allow students to act on their learning and, in turn, learn from and reflect on their actions and engagements in the "real world" context.

WILL* intentionally weaves together the understanding and implementation of intersectionality with bridging theory and praxis to create an overarching program structure that teaches students how to critically evaluate social justice problems and take action toward addressing those problems.

As the director and associate director of WILL*, we have had the opportunity to oversee the program for nearly forty years collectively. That is a lot of time to think about and do the work of explicitly connecting theoretical inquiries in WGSS, queer studies, and critical race theory to praxis. Although incredibly fulfilling and inspiring, our jobs can be challenging. Helping a diverse group of young people work together to understand concepts like power, privilege, oppression, and intersectionality, not only at the level of the individual but also at the level of systems and institutions, is complex. We must continually examine our own positionality, knowledge, and assumptions as we learn from our students, one another, and new work in the field. We firmly believe that participation in the WILL* program encourages lifelong commitments to the hard, messy work of activism. As the following collection of stories demonstrates, our students recognize how important it is to engage in difficult conversations, push for increased equity, and create more just communities.

Key Elements of the WILL* Program

Before moving on to the stories contained within this book, it's important for us to highlight four elements that we have found most critical to the success of the WILL* program and our students. All four elements build on the program's critical frameworks of intersectionality and bridging theory and praxis. Not only are these elements important for educators to consider if they are interested in creating or expanding their own program, they are also, we believe, essential to a transformative student experience. As well, they provide important context for the stories that follow, as some of them will specifically reference the structure of the program. The four key elements are:

1. Building a community of diverse students. WILL*
members reflect a broad range of differences and identities that include but are not limited to race, ethnicity,
class, sexuality, gender identity, ability, religion, national
origin, and political beliefs. Of course, cultivating a
diverse membership by itself is not enough to create
community. Community creation takes intentional effort
inside and outside of the classroom. Students reflect the
contexts and communities in which they live; it takes
time and education to identify and challenge learned stereotypes and biases in order to build long-term trust and
understanding. This work takes patience, perseverance,
and dialogue, but community building cannot be successful without deliberate efforts to weave intersectional
thinking and action throughout its fabric.

2. Teaching inclusive leadership. The student leadership
organization, which one alum calls "the window into
the heart of the program," is one of the key features that
distinguishes membership in WILL*; it is more than completing a major or minor in WGSS. This dedicated space
for students creates community, engenders leadership, and
offers a structure conducive to activism. For example, one
student took the tools she gained from the student leadership organization and implemented a leadership program
for HIV-positive girls in Rwanda. The key to successful
student leadership is making it inclusive. As with community creation, we have learned that this is not something
that simply happens. Inclusive leadership must be continually taught, practiced, and reinforced. Students must
figure out a system to implement their understanding of
intersectionality, to recognize how overlapping systems of
oppression and privilege work in their daily lives. Attention to intersectionality forces students to think about
the organization's structure, programming, and mission.
They think about what kind of messaging, both implicit

and explicit, the organization creates. They also generate ground rules and learn how to work with each other when someone violates those rules. Students learn to speak up, listen to one another, and become better able to recognize whose voices are not being heard or are absent altogether. This work enables students to better walk the talk of intersectionality by challenging one another to do the hard work of addressing deep-seated systems of oppression and being aware of how these systems affect everyday individual and group dynamics.[20]

3. Valuing mentorship. As the directors of WILL*, we serve as mentors to every student, meeting with them individually, advising the student leadership team, and teaching several of their required courses. We fully believe that the best learning happens when teachers work side-by-side with their students and bring them, as fully as possible, into every aspect of their work. As bell hooks notes, "students want us to see them as whole human beings with complex lives and experiences rather than simply as seekers after compartmentalized bits of knowledge."[21] WILL* is a testament to ongoing dialogue and change based on ever-evolving student needs and passions. Upper-class students provide first- and second-year students with guidance and direction. Faculty and staff across the university serve as advisers and teachers to our students. And scholars, activists, and performers who come to campus as part of the WILL*/WGSS annual speaker series work with students in small groups and workshops, in addition to their public talks and performances.

These events outside of the classroom work hand-in-hand with the WILL* curriculum to create integrative learning experiences. Not only are they important for students' individual development and success, but they also spark campus-wide discussion, and often action, on important social justice issues. As one of our members writes in regard to the speaker series: "Each year when the lineup would be announced, I would look at the list of speakers thinking, *No Beyoncé, again? I don't know any of these people.* While I didn't know them before their talks, I now can tell you how compelling their messages were. What the speaker series provided me most was a glimpse into the many issues that were so beyond the horizon of my mind at the time."

4. Creating a unique, student-centered space. Our program model works in large part because students occupy different types of spaces with one another. The classroom space of WGSS gives them a foundational, shared knowledge base from which to better analyze the world around them. Yet it alone does not give them a place outside of the classroom to build an intentional community with accountability to one another and the ability to develop leadership skills. WILL* does. Collective experiences both in and out of the classroom build a shared, activist-oriented intellectual community among students. The student leadership organization, the small group meetings with guest speakers, and the many opportunities to connect theory and praxis encourage students to make informed decisions and act on them.

The program is intentionally designed to offer students space not only to succeed in their work, but also to fail; it helps them learn to practice resiliency and address inevitable setbacks. And, perhaps not surprisingly, their participation in this shared, student-centered space results in deep connections and close friendships with one another across four years in the program and often for many years afterwards. As one graduate writes, "Years later now, when something outrageous happens in the world, I know that I can pick up a phone, call a former WILL* member and say, 'Hold on, I'm not losing my mind, right? This is really outrageous, right?'"

How Feminist Collaboration Created This Book

One of our main goals in sharing the twelve stories in this book is to share the power of the WILL* program because we know the impact it has on young people. But the process of writing the book involved a number of starts and stops before we figured out our way forward. In short, making this book has been messy. We first interviewed twenty-four graduates, people we knew had powerful stories, unique life experiences, and something important to relay to a larger audience.

After conducting these interviews, we chose which stories to include. We tried to think across not only the diversity of identities but also the diversity of experiences. We prioritized particularly unique and compelling stories—which was hard, because the stories of everyone we interviewed could have easily been included using this measure.

Next, we began to write the twelve stories based on our interview transcripts. But we quickly realized that this method was not going to work. We could not get them quite right. Or right at all. The process of trying to write in these individuals' voices while not actually being them felt at best, inauthentic and at worst, fraudulent. While the problem was partly that we did not have enough interview material to tell the full story, we also simply couldn't get the voice right. Our attempts to write all of them in the same voice and tone cheapened them somehow. The personalities of the storytellers fell flat, as did the dynamism and passion of the stories themselves, the very stories we had been so energized by when we first heard them.

So we rethought our process. With some trepidation, since we had already taken several hours of people's time in order to complete the interviews, we asked our selected alums if they would consider writing their own stories. We offered them their interview transcripts, our notes on their interviews, and a detailed outline of the "through line" we saw in their stories.

We asked a lot in asking them to write their stories themselves; this new process involved numerous back-and-forth conversations as we took on new roles as editors curating a story collection, something we had not initially imagined.

In the end, it worked. Authentic voice returned as each story took on the personality of its author. While the clock kept ticking and the creation of the book became more and more prolonged, this process of feminist consensus and working in deep collaboration to generate each story felt both genuine and constructive. While we certainly sacrificed a quick timeline and an easier editorial process by pursuing this method, the result—a truly collaborative work—was worth it.

In the pages that follow, twelve authors speak to the activist work being done all around us. They represent diverse identities across race, sexuality, gender identity, nationality, and age. They have pursued different professional and personal paths in their lives. Some are in the legal field, others in science and non-profits. Some have a life partner; some don't. Some have children; some don't. And they highlight different sets of skills and experiences from the WILL* program that have proven most valuable in their lives, underscoring how the takeaways and lifelong learning from the program vary based on individual experience. You will discover, however, that they all agree that their participation in the program encouraged them to develop an enduring commitment to the work of creating a more just and equitable society.

As Marshall Ganz writes, the best stories help us understand age-old questions of: "What am I called to do? What is my community called to do? And what are we called to do *now*?"[22] The best stories, in other words, engage both our heads and our hearts. They help us translate our values into everyday practice. And perhaps most importantly, they motivate us to action.[23]

We hope these stories serve this function for you. If they do and you are reading this book as an educator or a student, we encourage you to think about how a program like WILL* might benefit your school. If you have WGSS classes, what might it mean to create a robust student organization dedicated to praxis? If you don't, could someone start teaching a social justice–oriented course that bridges theoretical knowledge with practical application outside of the classroom? Maybe your school has those courses hiding under other names. Or maybe you can help organize folks, either from your position as an educator or a student, to create demand for this type of coursework. If you are doing similar work, and we know many of you are, we would love to hear from you. If you want to be doing something like WILL* at your school and you think we could help, we definitely want to chat.

We want these stories to either encourage you to engage in social justice work or to sustain you in the work you are already doing. Social justice work is hard work, and sometimes we get so overwhelmed that we don't know where to start or we get so bogged down in the process that we can't see the good we are accomplishing. We hope these stories remind you of the power and rewards of this work.

As you read these stories, keep the following themes in mind. Not only do they capture the power of the WILL* program, but they also frame the importance of these concepts in doing social justice work more generally. Most of the stories speak to several of these themes, further demonstrating their centrality to sustained activism. These themes are:

- *Authenticity.* Several of our authors speak to the importance of living one's values. Emily Miller learned to embrace being both a member of the LGBTQ community and her church community. Lisa Gray speaks about the importance of not letting the judgment of others prevent her from doing what's best for her life. Shavari Dalal-Dheini discusses the importance of being genuinely herself, especially within a marriage.

Second, our academic foundation has both shifted and expanded. When the program was founded in 1980, the students involved earned a minor in women's studies, an academic discipline that grew directly out of the women's movement.[25] Some alums will refer to their minor in women's studies. While women's studies programs initially focused on theories and histories of women, over time they expanded tremendously to interrogate constructions of gender and sexuality, as well as concepts like intersectionality, much more broadly. Like many other colleges and universities, the University of Richmond renamed its women's studies program in 2004 to women, gender, and sexuality studies (WGSS) to better capture the diverse work being done in the field. This more expansive designation allows for courses examining not only women but also masculinities, transgender studies, queer studies, critical race studies, and more. Our more recent graduates refer to their minor in WGSS.

Now, to the stories. First, you will hear from Allison Speicher, class of 2008. We start with Allison because she nicely sets the stage for the rest of the stories as she moves between her narrative and the foundational frameworks of the program. From there, the stories follow in chronological order based on the author's year of graduation. Cammie Dunaway, who graduated in 1984 as part of WILL*'s first graduating class, will be next. The collection ends with Jah Akande, class of 2013. Enjoy.

CHAPTER 1:
Allison

Allison Speicher, class of 2008, is an educator and writer who recently published the book Schooling Readers, *which investigates the intersections of education, literature, and activism. The academic component of WILL*, including the required internship, taught her that the inequalities she witnessed while student teaching in an under-resourced school in Richmond, Virginia "could be a means of praxis, personal transformation, and social activism." In her current position at Eastern Connecticut State University teaching first-generation college students and future teachers like herself, she is dedicated to addressing entrenched educational inequities. She strives to make her own classroom a "liberatory space of possibility and action."*

When I came to the University of Richmond as a very scared scholarship student with something to prove, I had never thought about what a feminist was and I certainly wouldn't have claimed the label for myself. I was just a smart girl with a history of activism, a penchant for speaking her mind, and a tendency to complain when we only read books by dead white men in English class. What did any of that have to do with feminism?

My first academic engagement with gender issues was in the WILL program. Within the first few weeks of class, it quickly dawned on me that not only was the F word not scary, it was something I had been practicing for an awfully long time.

I came to Richmond knowing I wanted to be a teacher, intending to study math and education, but that changed quickly, too. I enrolled in Women in Modern Literature, a class for my women, gender, and sexuality studies (WGSS) minor, with Dr. Suzanne Jones, a professor who would alter my vision of myself and my future profoundly. Dr. Jones's class was hard, and she was tough. She had this annoying habit of asking endless follow-up questions, and when I went to her office hours to work on my writing, she had equally endless suggestions for revision. This was a brave new world for a young woman accustomed to lavish praise. Yet, despite my discomfort, the way I felt when I trudged out of Calculus II could not compare to the vigor and energy that raced through me every time I entered the English department. Within a matter of weeks, I was an English major.

Fast-forward ten years: I'm an English professor myself, and Suzanne Jones is still my mentor.

In Dr. Jones's class and in my other WGSS classes, I was exposed to something new—to feminist theory, to women's cultural productions, to individuals who thought about gender with cogency and conviction. But this something new was also something intimately familiar. I was acquiring a vocabulary to describe what was at stake in those heated conversations I had with my grandmother about what it meant to be female and valedictorian or with other family members about women working outside the home. I also was acquiring a framework that helped me understand what I had fallen passionately in love with in the books that had formed the center of my childhood, books like *Little Women*. Jo March was like me, only better. She was rebellious, but longed to be good; kind, but unrefined; fierce, but compassionate. Most importantly, she struggled to find a path for herself in the midst of strict gender expectations, unwilling to let others make her decisions and eager to use her pen to find her voice.

When I later became a scholar of Alcott's work and, more broadly, nineteenth-century American literature—thanks, once again, to Dr. Jones—I would finally appreciate just how important *Little Women* is to literary history. And that, of course, means I get to incorporate *Little Women* into every single course I teach. Thank you, Ms. Alcott, for this incredible gift, and thank you, WILL, for helping me to unwrap it.

The knowledge and vocabulary I gained in my WGSS classes didn't just help me to excel in my English classes, become a scholarly writer, and contextualize my own childhood. WILL was integral to the development of my pedagogy and teaching philosophy. By the time I got to Richmond, I knew firsthand what teachers could do, because they had done it for me. My teachers had reflected back to me a kinder, more insightful, and more accomplished version of myself and then helped me to become the person they believed me to be. And I knew teaching was right for me because I had been doing it all my life. Most importantly, I believed the classroom could be a safe and transformative space in which we could change ourselves, and in doing so, change the world.

So I embarked on a minor in education. I took a variety of classes that taught me some very, very useful things, like how to write a lesson plan that keeps students awake and how to use quality instruction to prevent disciplinary issues. And I learned some less useful things, like where best to put your pencil sharpener. Today, I draw on the methods I learned constantly and still hear the voice of my amazing education professor, Ms. Kimberlye Joyce, in my head when I'm faced with difficult split-second teaching decisions.

But what I didn't learn in my teacher education program was how to meet the needs of my students and keep my sanity in the kind of environment in which I wished to teach.

As a first-generation college student myself, I was drawn to underserved student populations, and as someone with years of activist experience, I passionately believed that if social justice were to be achieved, it would be achieved, at least in part, in the classroom. There's a reason schools are so often on the frontlines of battles for racial equality. Just picture six-year-old Ruby Bridges on the steps of William Franz Elementary School or the Little Rock Nine, and you'll see what I mean.

While I took a course on "diverse learners and environments," it left me with little preparation to handle the challenges of student teaching in the impoverished, majority African American high school where I requested placement, hoping I was ready to act on my beliefs. Ultimately, what preparation I had for my time at this school I gained from WILL. I came to the school with an intellectual understanding of systems of inequality, knowing that even though schools can be agents of change, that doesn't mean they somehow exist outside these systems. WILL helped me to diagnose what I saw in my classroom: the way racism and classism in particular shaped every facet of our school environment, from the expectations placed on the students to the opportunities denied them. WILL also taught me that the things I saw and the way they made me feel could be a means of praxis, personal transformation, and social activism.

But knowing that didn't make it easier to feel and see what I felt and saw. Barely twenty-one years old, I arrived at the school with a burning desire to prove myself and make a difference, dressed in clothes that I hoped made me look at least five years older. On my first day there, I was ushered into my classroom, a fifty-two-foot by thirteen-foot single-wide trailer parked in front of the school building in what our principal euphemistically referred to as the "academic village." The trailer had a single center aisle that my students would come to call "Spice's catwalk" in my honor, and was equipped with fifteen work tables and thirty chairs—an especially appropriate number, considering the fact that several of my classes had thirty-four students. The school is near an airport, and the flight path went over my trailer. Every time a plane took off, the entire structure shook and no one could hear what anyone else was saying. I remember asking where the bathroom trailer was, given our distance from the school building, and I was calmly assured that there would never again be a bathroom trailer, since a student had set it on fire the previous year.

Needless to say, this was a less than ideal educational environment, not at all what I'd been taught to picture in the education course I'd taken where we'd drawn sample classroom maps. Worse still, the students knew that other schools didn't look like ours. They read the situation correctly; they knew the powers that be didn't think it was important for them to have an adequate classroom because they didn't think the students themselves were important. One of the most heartrending conversations I had with a student was about the school environment. He remarked: "Big S, I used to think you were smart, but then somebody told me you chose to come here, so you must be stupid." I have no idea what I said back, probably because there was nothing to say.

I had little opportunity to reflect on these issues in my first hours at the school, however, because I had faculty development to attend. During my first week, I was issued important equipment: a camo-print kazoo, which I was instructed to use to whistle at troublemakers when on deck duty (akin to hall duty), and a camo-print T-shirt with the words "Mission Impossible: No mission is too great" printed upon it. No one felt the need to inform me why it was a good idea for the faculty to announce to the students that we found the task of educating them to be impossible. The distribution of these camo-print prizes was only a prelude to the real highlight: a meeting of all the faculty at which the administrators appeared in fatigues and boots and challenged the teachers to a relay race. After the race, we marched around the school, and then received Army lanyards for our keys and Army calendars for our bulletin boards.

Little did I know that when I had signed on to teach twelfth graders the English canon from *Beowulf* to Chaucer, I had also signed on to participate in military recruitment. But this was central to the school's culture. My mentor teacher would spend parent-teacher conferences, on those rare occasions when parents were able to come, telling parents how well their children would do in the armed forces, while I kept inviting the students to write practice college application essays. Our basic school supplies, like pencils, were supplied by military recruiters, who were a regular presence on campus. I should add here that I'm sure many of my students went on to do well in the military, that it gave them opportunities. But I believe that education should enlighten young people about all the opportunities available to them and that those who choose to enter the military should be free to make that decision without the pressure of their teachers.

The militarization of my high school's culture impeded my ability to create open, nonhierarchical classrooms focused on academic learning, personal growth, and individual choice. When one of my students who planned to join the Marines refused to write his college essay assignment, I pushed him to write an essay instead about why he chose the Marines and what this choice meant to him. He plagiarized the Wikipedia entry for the Marines, and when I pointed this out and asked him to rewrite it, the school authorities decided instead to move him to a "less writing-intensive" English class. This student was destined for the armed forces, so, by their logic, why did he need academic rigor? Several years later, I'm still disgusted by this story—both by the implication that those in the military do not benefit from strong literacy skills and by the fact that the militarized culture of the school became an excuse not to have high expectations for every student. It also made me profoundly uncomfortable because the vast majority of my students were African American, a group represented disproportionately in the armed forces. Let's just say that when I did practicum in majority white and middle-class schools, there was no camouflage and no marching.

From my first hours at the school, I was indoctrinated into this school culture. Within the first week, I became determined to change that culture, at least within my own classroom. I learned, first and foremost, to keep my eyes and ears open and to get to know my students as well as possible. No amount of academic knowledge could have prepared me for what I saw and heard. Many of my students were responsible for raising siblings or their own children; many lacked reliable emotional and financial support from their adult guardians. Most held jobs outside of school. Many were food-insecure. Few had any real knowledge about sex or protection; many had the unintended pregnancies to prove it. Gang violence was a major component of their lives. I remember a series of tear-filled conversations with one of my students in which my mentor teacher and I begged the student not to try to avenge his brother's death and lose his own life in the process. His brother had been shot and killed after being mistaken for a gang member the previous year. This student was one of the most charismatic and genuinely affectionate people I have ever met, and I'll never forget how his smile could make his classmates and me forget we were in a single-wide trailer being rocked by airplanes. These students rarely wore their scars on their sleeves, but it was almost impossible to teach them without trying to figure out the context of their lives.

This, then, was the challenge before me: how to teach a curriculum filled with poetry by dead white men to students accustomed to low expectations, living lives rife with violence and uncertainty, suffering from hunger, working to support themselves, and trying to navigate adult relationships without adults to lean on for support and guidance.

Some steps were easy. I stocked a small classroom food pantry. I also customized our curriculum to allow us to discuss topics important to the students' lives. *Beowulf*, for example, really is in part about turf warfare, and I asked my students to adapt scenes from the poem into a present-day context, which got us talking about violence and what motivates it. When we read *The Canterbury Tales*, I asked students to write their own prologue introducing representative travelers from our time period, which led to important discussions about careers and consumerism. Continually amazed by the students' lack of knowledge about sexuality, I turned a lesson on *The Canterbury Tales* in which a woman's "maidenhead" is taken from her by force into a lesson on consent and respect. Alarmed by the gender dynamic of our classroom, which extended to the students' treatment of me, I turned a lesson on poetry into a lesson on gender. We compared and contrasted the images of women in poetry, exposing how thinking about womanhood is frequently contradictory and pejorative. I ended that class by choosing the female student most in need of Maya Angelou to read "Phenomenal Woman" aloud.

I strove desperately to improve the students' writing skills, obviously neglected over the course of their educations, and invited them all to come in for help during lunch. All in all, on the academic side, we made the most of what we had, and what we had was twelve copies of *The Canterbury Tales* for 150 students.

Finding ways to make the curriculum more responsive to my students' lives and needs was the easy part. Opening my heart to my students was easy, too. But living with the results, with the feelings, wasn't, particularly when I attended seminars with other student-teachers and heard that the biggest problems their schools faced were helicopter parents or not enough video cameras for every student. I developed relationships with these students at a level of intensity I will probably never again experience, and I thank them for all the ways in which they educated me about what it means to be a teacher.

One particular student still weighs heavily on my mind and heart. I hope she's okay and alive and fabulous; I hope

they all are. I caught her neglecting her *Beowulf* worksheet
one day, writing something on the back instead. Rather than
busting her, I asked to see what she had written. It was a
poem, a pretty good one. I asked her if I could turn it in to
the school literary magazine and if she'd like to keep working
on her writing with me during her study hall. We ended up
spending third block together every other day, talking, not
talking, writing, not writing, and eating granola. One day, I
was grading one of her assignments and caught a reference to
killing herself. I notified my mentor teacher and the guidance
department, and when she came back to visit with me the
next day, we talked about my concern for her. Essentially, I
learned, she had been testing me to see if I would care. She
later told me I was the first teacher she ever liked because I
was the first to really care about her. She was in twelfth grade.
I cried all the way home, on my long, forty-five-minute drive
to the safe, white, rich part of town.

What do you do with that kind of heartbreak? WILL
provided me with the means to try to process these feelings,
to share them with others, to use them to do some kind of
good. Since my student teaching was also my WILL internship, I compiled a journal reflecting on my experiences, using
the lenses I had learned in WGSS classes to try to understand
them. Rereading this journal several years and a PhD later,
I'm struck by how much I still feel and think like this twenty-
one-year-old—how much I still struggle to understand. One
passage in particular stands out:

> *When people ask me how student teaching is going, I
> often do not know what to tell them. I long to ask, Do
> you want the generic "fine" or the truth? Do you want
> to know that this experience has been both the most
> empowering and the most painful experience of my life?
> Do you want to know that I am physically exhausted
> but when I go to sleep, many nights I lie awake thinking
> about my students' problems? Do you want to hear*

*about my students' strength in facing adversity? Are
you prepared to be mobilized against the adversity they
face? Do you want me to smile and say this is a great
opportunity for me, or to tell you that I will never be the
same again? Do you want me to tell you that I'm making
a difference, or that this is so overwhelmingly larger than
me that the phrase "making a difference" rings hollow?*

The sentence that strikes me, the sentence that reminds
me never to underestimate my own twenty-one-year-old
students, is the last one. It raises two key questions: 1) Did
anything I do at my school matter? and 2) Why did other
people seem bent on insisting that it did? I remember becoming very suspicious of anyone who tried to praise the work
I was doing, very angry that they had such a sanguine view
of how easy it would be to overcome educational inequality
and a self-satisfied sense that just knowing someone who was
doing something was almost the same as doing something
oneself. I'm not sure if this was a fair assessment of many of
the people in my life—in fact, I'm sure it was not—but my
anger stemmed from a deeper sense that the message our
culture sends is that educational inequality will be fixed one
bleeding-heart, white, middle-class heroine at a time.

What I love about WILL, one of the most important
gifts it gave to me, is the sense that it's okay to be this angry,
that it might even be *right* to be this angry, because anger
can make stuff happen. Being brokenhearted can make stuff
happen. Emotions and praxis walk hand in hand. I'm better
for this anger; I'm a better teacher, a better ally. I've done a
number of things in my life post-Richmond that I probably
wouldn't have without this anger, including getting involved
in bridge programs that help underserved students transition to college. WILL gave me a platform to reflect on my
story and my students' stories and to share them, to share my
meager understanding of what took place and my overwhelming sense that I will never really understand it.

I remember being invited to speak about my student teaching, and a senior university administrator came up to talk with me after the event with tears still in his eyes. Those tears meant something to me, and they still do. Maybe I've been heavily influenced by the nineteenth-century female authors I study, many of whom believed getting an affective response from their readers was necessary for creating social change, but I truly believe that making others feel differently is a crucial step in helping them to think and act differently.

Looking back, I think that I accomplished a great deal at my high school and yet nothing at all. I hope that some of my students' lives are better because I was a small part of them; I know my own is richer and deeper because of what we shared. But it wasn't enough. Individual change in individual classrooms will never be enough to erase the damage racism and classism have done to schools and the young people who populate them. Only systemic change can. But systemic change only happens when enough people change and open their minds, when inequality becomes visible and visceral, and thus intolerable. WILL and student teaching taught me that message, and my life experiences have only reinforced it.

And that's what I do now as a college professor: I help to change how people think. I create the opportunity and environment to help people evolve in their understandings of race, class, gender, and sexuality, and to challenge me to evolve in my own. Some people may blame me for choosing to leave K–12, may see my decision as running away from a problem instead of trying to solve it. Some days, I am one of those people. But I had started my graduate school applications before I ever set foot in that trailer, and I wasn't ready to end being a student.

If a student were to ask me which path to follow in life, I would advise her to try to find a career and a setting that would allow her to capitalize on all of her strengths, to flourish and live a life of meaning. WILL taught me that lesson, and that's the choice I made for myself by going to graduate school. The most difficult thing I've ever done in my life wasn't teaching at an impoverished school. It was deciding to leave it.

After leaving, I continued to think—and still do—of my trailer, and the life I might have had there, with guilt and grief and fondness. It would be a long time before I would stumble upon the words that would be a balm to my troubled soul. It was just a few years ago, in fact, that I came across William Alcott's *Confessions of a Schoolmaster*, published in 1839. (And yes, he *is* related to Louisa May.) It's an insightful and remarkably relevant read, the reflections of a truly reflective practitioner. At the end of the memoir, Alcott leaves teaching to become a medical doctor, and he does so with regret. But his memoir ends triumphantly: "though I do not move, at all times, in the same particular sphere, I am, at all times and under all circumstances, a friend of common schools—ready to be a sacrifice, if need be, to their welfare."[1]

Though to many twenty-first-century readers this sentence might seem overly melodramatic, when I read it, I felt like a kindred spirit was reaching out to me across a chasm nearly two centuries wide. Being a "friend" to public education is a personal and lifelong commitment, not a job title but an elemental part of one's being, inside the classroom or outside it. Though I will always admire those who work with all their hearts at schools like the one where I taught, I know now that I didn't need to spend my life in that trailer in order to work for educational equality and inclusivity in the classroom.

Because of my training in education, I came to graduate school aware that mass public education is a product of nineteenth-century activism. Because of my training in literature, I knew that most nineteenth-century reform causes inspired fiction. I put two and two together and decided to look for common school fictions, confident that education reform must have been immortalized in a story or two—or, as I soon found out, a hundred or so. This research, which started as my dissertation and is now a book, was deeply rooted in my experiences as a student teacher and as a WILL woman.

In my classroom, my students continuously asked me, "Why do we have to be here?" While this question seems to reek of juvenile angst, in a school neglected and discarded and populated by students who had been devalued and forgotten, it was a genuine question, one I wasn't sure I could answer. What I found when I started reading common school narratives is that they ask this same question. Written at the foundational moment of mass public education, they openly debate just what schooling is, what it's for, and whom it serves. Is schooling meant to ensure social stability or enhance social mobility? Do schools serve the individual, the community, or the nation? What is gained by getting an education? What is lost? Reading these has made me a far more reflective teacher, continually questioning what my work in the classroom means in ways I find invigorating, not debilitating. And I know that these questions are still worth asking today, not only because of what I have read but also because of what I have lived.

As a college teacher today, I am the kind of teacher whom students routinely call quirky, the kind of teacher who inevitably assigns too much reading and who believes deeply in the transformative power of the classroom. When I think of what I want my classroom to be like, WILL comes to mind. I want to build a community that encourages disagreement rather than groupthink, to provide a safe space that is also deeply challenging, to develop relationships with students that support who they are now as well as who they can become.

Many of the courses I have taught have been inspired by WGSS. For example, the first class I designed was called "Sugar and Spice and Everything Nice." For fifteen weeks, I challenged first-year students to contemplate the figure of the tomboy: her liberatory potential, her entanglement with systems of inequality, her history, and her future. My supervisor visited the class and remarked, "I love the atmo-sphere of this class. It's like they need to be here. It's like this class fills a need." I think she was exactly right. The students in the class were hungry, hungry for the concepts they were learning, the thinking they were doing, the conversations we were having. I frequently describe this class as feeling like an intellectual slumber party, a chance to be comfort-able with people you trust while having deeply meaningful conversations, which isn't a bad description of WILL. It was also a class that surprised students. For example, one student candidly remarked on her course evaluation that she hadn't realized how much the course would challenge her unac-knowledged homophobia.

That first class directly inspired the next class I designed. A student came to my office in a frenzy one afternoon, deeply upset about an event she had just experienced at the business school. From what I understood, the student had participated in a values auction, in which students had a certain amount of capital to spend on what they wanted out of life, from a nice house to a comfortable retirement to a loving spouse and kids. She was upset that her female classmates had bent over back-wards to publicly demonstrate that they valued marriage and children most highly while her male peers sat and watched. "I just knew you'd understand," she exclaimed, making me wonder just how she'd deduced that I was a proud spinster. (And if you think "spinster" is pejorative, by the way, look up the word's history.)

From this conversation, I developed the course "All the Single Ladies: Representations of Single Women from Spin-ster to Sex Kitten." This class challenged students to think carefully not only about what psychologist Bella DePaulo calls "matrimania" but also about what they want out of life, what choices they will make in the future, and how these choices should be *choices*, not inevitabilities. I helped these students to master the vocabulary I'd gained from WILL, and to see that we can value one another's choices, even when those choices are different. And they helped me to think more deeply about being single and the ways in which our cultural discussions of marriage are shaped as much by sexism and homophobia as they are by love and loyalty.

What I learned in WILL continues to shape my classroom practice, as does my student teaching experience. At both my graduate and current institution, I've taught in bridge programs that help underserved and first-generation students transition to college. I hope, when I am working with these students, that I am living up to my promise to my high school students never to forget our time together—or as they put it, to "keep it hood." Programs like these give me hope that more students like those I taught so many years ago will find their way to college environments in which they can flourish and experience education as a tool of self-discovery and personal fulfillment. This is what I want for all my students. I know that schools and teachers can wound or heal, beat down or uplift, bore or excite, reinforce inequality or challenge it. I hope that as a teacher, I sow the seeds of courage, intellectual acuity, diligence, self-love, and social responsibility, and that my students will reap the harvest.

In many ways, the story of my evolution as a teacher has now come full circle. I am now an assistant professor of English at Eastern Connecticut State University, a university committed to extending access to higher education and providing a diverse range of students with a "liberal education, practically applied," as our slogan proclaims. I teach literature courses that include classes designed to meet the needs of future teachers in particular—a rather serendipitous way to remain a "friend" of public schooling, and one I never foresaw in the days I spent mourning the life I left behind. I see in so many of my students the same enthusiasm and fear I felt when I was a student of education. I hope that I can complement the skills and support the education professors give them, and that I can provide them with a safe place to vent, a shoulder to cry on, and, most importantly, the tools and opportunities they need to process and contextualize their experiences. That's what WILL provided for me.

WGSS didn't teach me to be a teacher. Richmond's education faculty did a tremendous job of that. But it did teach me the critical and analytical skills I needed to strive for the ever-elusive goal of becoming a reflective practitioner. My research helped me to develop this skill further, to be able to place my classroom work within the context of two hundred years of education history.

Teaching is a philosophically and emotionally complicated job—and so is being a student. I hope I can provide all of my students with the opportunity to consider seriously what it means to seek and to gain an education. Doing so requires continuous interrogation into systems of inequality in all of the courses I teach. My story ends at a beginning. I've taught many students, and I aim to teach many, many more. For each, I hope to provide something like the WILL experience—a transformative moment that will help them to understand that right now, education is a privilege, but it needn't be that way forever, and we all have a role to play in helping others gain access to and agency within that magical place we call the classroom. But for now, I'll end this story here; after all, I have lesson plans to write.

CHAPTER 2:

Cammie

Cammie Dunaway, class of 1984, is a member of WILL*'s first graduating class. When WILL* began, it emphasized leadership and community, two themes that endure today. Cammie earned her MBA from Harvard and went on to become a top executive at Yahoo and Nintendo, consistently prioritizing learning and change over comfort and stasis. Within the male-dominated spaces of the corporate world, she challenges traditional notions of success to ensure that her work reflects her own values, even when doing so has entailed changing jobs. Cammie also cultivates lifelong friendships and partnerships—the kinds of relationships that, she feels, best offer fulfillment and happiness. She is the coauthor of the recently released book Fit Matters: How to Love Your Job.

I grew up with a poster on the lavender walls of my girlhood bedroom of a soaring ballerina and the words "if you can dream it, you can become it." Even with that daily reminder and with two loving parents who placed a high value on education and experience, my world and my dreams were pretty predictable. You know, the stuff of many small-town Southern girls in the 1970s: make the cheerleading squad, date a handsome boy, and make good enough grades to get into college. I actually chose my college, the University of Richmond, in part because of the lovely buildings and landscaping. I even had fantasies about a handsome boy proposing to me someday in the gazebo by Westhampton Lake.

Then, a few months before I left for college, a post-card arrived that ultimately led me to reach for much bigger dreams. The University of Richmond was starting a new program called WILL (Women Involved in Living and Learning). The card said it would encompass some classroom time, workshops, and enrichment opportunities. It emphasized that participants would learn more about themselves and issues that impact women's lives. It promised an avenue to creating a sense of community with women on campus.

The idea of self-exploration seemed interesting; to this day, I'm a sucker for those personality self-assessments you see in magazines. I've also always been a bit of a "joiner." So I filled out the card and, three months later, found myself in the company of the twelve other young women who made up WILL's first class. Over the next four years, my worldview and my dreams got much larger and more vibrant. My confidence and ability to reach for those dreams grew as well.

Some people may be born with the ability to envision life outside of what they have been exposed to, but I think for most of us, our dreams are shaped by what we read about, talk about, and experience. WILL introduced me to a new world of successful women who had shaped our history through their audacious visions: Susan B. Anthony daring to demand voting rights for women, Marie Curie dreaming that a woman could win a Nobel Prize, Ella Baker organizing for civil rights, and Billie Jean King demonstrating that she could play tennis on the same level as the guys.

For each of these women, achieving started with taking the limits off of what they aspired to accomplish, and certainly not stopping with what others deemed appropriate. So I started to envision getting a job with the best advertising agency in the region and going to the world's top business school. Later, I envisioned making $100,000 a year (at the time an almost unthinkable sum), starting a business with my husband, and moving across the country to take a new job in an entirely new industry. Most recently, I have been envisioning a life with a better blend of professional accomplishment and personal fulfillment. But I learned that the first step to success is taking the limits off of what you dare to believe is possible.

Through WILL, I was not only exposed to historic role models, but I was also given the opportunity to interact with a diverse set of vibrant female role models on campus. In high school, some wonderful female teachers had inspired me, but they tended to be shaped from the same mold: English teachers, passionate about literature, beautifully dressed, and married with families. They were dedicated professionals, but all professional in a startlingly similar way.

The WILL program turned that model on its head. Suddenly I was interacting with a group of successful professors who shared little in common, other than being female and having a commitment to their field of study and their students. There was Dr. Kathleen Rohaly, professor of physical education, who was funny and straightforward, taught courses on human sexuality, and was an outspoken LGBTQ ally. Dr. Jane Hopkins, director of the Women's Resource Center, was always polished and professional, the ultimate working mom. Dr. Jill Hunter was young, accessible, and finding her own way in her career. Finally, there was Dr. Stephanie Bennett, the dean of Westhampton and founder of WILL. Dr. Bennett was a smart and demanding yet unfailingly gracious woman, a woman so committed to her dreams of education for young women that she lived thousands of miles away from her husband. That sort of life choice was shockingly rare at the time.

From these women, I learned that success does not come dressed in a certain way or with any particular degree.

I started to understand that success comes when you pay attention to your own voice and desires and have the courage to pursue the path of your heart rather than let yourself be swayed by the expectations of others.

I am particularly thankful for these University of Richmond women because as I moved along in my career, it was rare to have these types of role models. More often than not, I was the most senior woman at the company and the only female in the room. With no daily corporate examples to follow, I relied on the strong foundation of female role models I had studied and observed through my four years of college. After all, if Elizabeth I could defeat the Spanish Armada, Margaret Sanger could revolutionize health care, and Shirley Chisholm could run for president, surely I could galvanize support for my team's project or command attention in a boardroom!

There was a freedom in our WILL classes to ask the tough questions, to speak without censure, to share our fears and weaknesses as well as our strengths. I don't know if it came from the skill of the professors, from only having women in the classroom, or from being together with the same group of students for four years. But it was there. And for me, it spilled over into my other classes as well. I went from being a girl who had done well but had not really stood out in high school to one who was taking challenging classes and making A's. I was stepping into student leadership positions. I was developing a view of myself as confident and capable that fuels me even now. While I have encountered plenty of challenges in my career, the underpinning belief that I can succeed and succeed on my own terms has sustained me even through trying times, as the following examples will illustrate:

- As a young advertising account executive, my client first mistook me for a secretary and second, presumed that as a secretary, I should get him a cup of coffee.

I told him who I was and graciously offered to get a cup for him as I filled my own. I realized that getting respect would require me to work harder and be more prepared than everyone else in the room. That same client eventually wrote a glowing recommendation for me when I decided to pursue my MBA.

- In deciding on a business school, I opted for Harvard Business School over choices that felt more comfortable because I knew the environment would push me further and that having credentials as a Harvard Business School MBA would open doors. It was a grueling two years that gave me mental toughness, as well as a valuable network that I still rely on today.

- At Frito-Lay, I left the familiarity of a cushy marketing job to run a route truck and lead a group of frontline sales guys. This ultimately led to a job where I managed $700 million in sales and nearly 1,000 employees.

- After thirteen years with PepsiCo, I moved my family across the country to take on a role in the relatively unknown world of the internet. Marketing was not a well-understood position at the company, and I spent as much time selling internally as externally. But gaining that digital expertise led to many new opportunities, including the public board positions I hold today.

Each of these choices was marked by a willingness to push beyond my comfort zone, to not settle for what felt expected or safe, and to prioritize learning over comfort. In each case, I was buoyed by a sense of confidence that went back to my WILL days, a sense that with hard work and courage, anything was possible.

Another of the life-shaping lessons of WILL was the value of having a safe place to express myself within a community of people who truly knew me. We were a fairly diverse group and not necessarily the closest of friends outside the program, but there was a deep sense of commitment and trust that came from our shared experience. I have tried to bring this into my career through encouraging a sense of authenticity at work. Simple things like having my team share personal wins as well as professional ones at each staff meeting have helped build this sense of community. I have also made a practice of putting my personal calendar commitments on my work calendar so that colleagues can see that I have a life outside of work. I try to take the time to know elements of each individual's life and goals outside of the job so that I can encourage them to pursue those passions. All of these things have helped me build an environment of trust at work. I am convinced that we do our best work when we feel comfortable bringing our whole selves into our jobs.

There have been times, however, when despite all my best efforts, it became clear that I could not bring my authentic self into the work environment. One job had all the right "optics"—prestige, big budget, great compensation, lots of perks—but lacked the cultural attributes of trust, empowerment, and accountability that have come to be important to me. I think of myself as a change agent, so I kept at it for several years, convinced that I could make a difference in the culture and unwilling to let go of what seemed to others like a perfect job. Then, one day, when I was speaking to a class of students, one of them asked me what was most important for career success and satisfaction. I quickly responded that for me, passion for the work and the mission of the company was key—but as I drove home a short time later, I realized that I was no longer following my own advice.

Shortly after that realization, I left for a job that was a much better fit for my style and desires. From that experience, I learned that you could have a good company and work for a good person but still not have a good fit. You always have some power to impact your work culture in positive ways, but you have to realize when the effort requires too much of a personal price and be willing to make a change.

Making that kind of change is much easier when you have economic flexibility and the support of friends and family. Just as my classmates in WILL provided honest feedback and formed a safe community in which I could explore new ideas and identities, my adult female friends have played a significant role in my ability to navigate difficult personal and professional situations. My girlfriends from Richmond have been a constant source of encouragement. We have lived through divorces, unemployment, losing parents, and the suicide of a close friend. Our every-other-year reunion serves as a touchstone for me: What has happened since the last time we were together? Am I on the road I want to be on? Am I being courageous in my life choices? It is no coincidence that some of my major life moves have come after a weekend with these women who know me so completely.

I have also had the fortune to have maintained several deep friendships from my early career days. As one moves up the ladder, it can be challenging to form close friendships at work, so I feel especially fortunate to have made these connections. These are women who can understand and advise me on things at work because they have been there too. One is a friend who was a young working mom like me when we met. I remember many Saturdays of taking our kids to a McDonald's playground, where we would sit with our computers, working and talking, sharing project challenges, frustrations, and advice. When you are a working mom, it is very hard to have any time left over for friendships, but friendships are essential to one's health and well-being and must be prioritized.

Also because I'm a working mom and an executive in a man's world, my husband has played a huge role in my success. We met when I responded to a personal ad, the only one he ever wrote and the only one I ever answered. He was looking for a "strong, independent woman in pursuit of her own dreams." My husband is smart, kind, generous, and talented. He has moved across the country three times for my career. He changed careers—from a more traditional corporate software engineer job to building out his own product design and manufacturing company—so that we would have stability at home even with my long hours and hectic travel schedule. Most essential, he has cheered me on when I have pursued my dreams and been there to pick me up when times were hard. We are partners in defining success as doing what gives us joy rather than following any prescribed path.

Being a mom has given me lots of joy and has made me a better, more empathetic leader, but it has also created many logistical challenges. I remember one of my mentors telling me not to have a child until I reached a director-level position. While I found the advice somewhat startling, it proved sound. Having a professional track record combined with a great support system at home made being a working mom possible. Family has served as the true north that has guided my decisions, clarified my perspective, and enhanced my life immeasurably.

A few years ago, as a means of finding better balance and fulfillment, I took a 30 percent pay cut and left a prestigious job to pursue an uncertain future in a small private company that had a mission I believed in. As that company's highest-ranking employee in the US, I had a chance to build out the kind of company I believed in *and* to be more autonomous in setting schedules and deliverables. I could see that being a mom of a teenager was actually more challenging and more time-consuming than being the mom of a toddler, so I valued the flexibility this job afforded me. It wasn't about professional sacrifice; it was about redefining a path to success.

Despite my joy and conviction about this opportunity, I have had to navigate a shift in some outside perceptions. A couple of years after taking the job, I realized that I had not received my usual invitation to *Fortune*'s annual Most Powerful Women Conference. Thinking there must have been a mistake, I sent a note to the organizers, who wrote back saying that they were sorry, but the event had become so popular that they needed to "cull the list." After having a small personal pity party over the fact that I no longer made the grade, I realized that this was an interesting call for self-reflection. Did I actually feel less powerful? I had gone from managing thousands of employees to working side by side with just a handful. Where I once oversaw a billion dollar budget, I now sweat over every one of my very limited dollars. No longer can I pick up the phone and call my head of human resources or information technology for instant expert analysis. I am now more likely to ask a question in an online forum and hope that someone out there has faced the same challenge. Maybe that's a lot less power.

Yet I have honestly never felt so engaged and confident. I am working on something that I believe can make a difference in the world. I am traveling to amazing places and getting to know people from different cultures. I have my hands back in creative tasks that I used to have to delegate. I only schedule meetings if something worthwhile is going to get accomplished. I can take my son to school and get home in time for dinner and bike rides with my family. Could it be that I have traded power for something deeper and more sustainable?

I have always been fascinated by the movement of people on and off *Fortune*'s Most Powerful Women list. It almost always seems that once a woman loses her position, she has lost her power and her place. Is this type of pressure really what all my WILL role models were fighting for? Is traditional power how women should define their success? Is that really what matters to our identity and happiness? It would be interesting to know if young businesswomen today aspire to be on a Most Powerful list or if they measure success by different yardsticks. My guess is that if they think about power, it is as a means to an end rather than an end in and of itself. Would a "Women Making the Biggest Difference" list look different? Or a list of "Women Enjoying Life the Most"?

Hopefully young women today are thinking and dreaming about power in new ways and will work to broaden the measures of success for us all.

I am grateful that WILL opened my eyes to my ability to achieve whatever level of success I could dream about and gave me the courage to define that success in terms of my choosing. As I enter the next phase of my own life and career, I plan to keep dreaming. I am eager to continue to learn and grow, and to contribute both to the people who are closest to me and to the larger world in ways that make a difference. I think my WILL role models would expect nothing less.

CHAPTER 3:

Lisa

Lisa Gray, class of 1993, credits the WILL* program with encouraging her to understand communities different from her own. It pushed her to work for more diverse and equitable educational and workspaces at the University of Richmond. Today, she remains committed to creating inclusive spaces in both her professional work at the University of Maryland Baltimore County (UMBC) and her mentoring relationships. As Lisa tells us, she strives for authenticity and integrity in both her personal and professional life.

When I think about how I became the person I am today, I always go back to my time at the University of Richmond and all that I experienced there, especially my involvement in the WILL program. My passion and commitment to diversity, social justice education, and activism started there.

As a teenager, I was always interested in the identities of other people. I had the sense that I really wanted to learn more about my own personal background and culture, too, but I didn't yet have the tools to do so. WILL was a continuation of those ideas that I had started to connect to in high school but didn't yet have the language to properly name.

When I got to college, my passion for what I now know as social justice work grew over time. Being a member of several historically underrepresented groups, I became acutely aware of what it meant to be marginalized. I felt it as a woman, I felt it as an African American student—one of just a few African American students on campus at the time—and I felt it as a member of the lower middle class. Though I didn't know how to name it, I saw how the economic advantages of some of my fellow classmates made their lives radically different from mine. I distinctly remember, for instance, looking at the parking lot behind my first-year residence hall and noticing all the cars in the lot and asking, "Wait, this lot is for first-year students? Why is that BMW parked there? How is that possible?"

Through WILL and the women's studies minor I earned, I began to analyze these early experiences with different and overlapping aspects of identity. I began to develop an idea of who I wanted to be professionally. I began to think of myself as a bridge builder, a person who helps different communities come together to connect and learn from each other. I took on leadership positions in different organizations, and I became known as that person who flowed through and across campus communities. No one could categorize me as being only with the Greek community, the minority students, or the theater people. This fluidity in my out-of-classroom involvements eventually led me to my WILL internship with Dr. Tina Cade and the Office of Multicultural Affairs (OMA).

My internship was a light bulb "aha" moment in terms of where I saw myself headed professionally. After thinking through a lot of different possibilities, I realized, "Wow, I can actually work on a college or university campus. I can work with students like me professionally!" Those early moments at the University of Richmond, coupled with WILL and my internship, opened up this previously unknown world to me. It all came together in my senior year as I developed a host of meaningful, cross-cultural relationships that helped me to see, among other things, the direction I wanted to take with my career.

I went on to earn my master's degree in higher education administration from Ohio State University, where I focused on leadership and diversity work. I interned at Otterbein College in the Office of Multicultural Affairs, which reinforced my desire to engage in diversity and inclusion work. After graduate school, I worked as a coordinator of multicultural programming in higher education, which led to a director position at the University of Baltimore. I then began doing diversity education from a management standpoint for the Maryland Motor Vehicle Administration. Though I learned a great deal in this new line of work, I desperately missed working with students and the vibrancy of a college campus. So, although the pay was better at the Motor Vehicle Administration, I returned to higher education. Currently, I serve as an associate director of student life with a focus on diversity and inclusion at the University of Maryland, Baltimore County.

I have learned that women, gender, and sexuality studies issues are much more complex and complicated than they are portrayed by some textbooks. For example, I now realize what was missing in some of my graduate school training—how different gender development can be for women of color and white women, for example, due to the impact of race, ethnicity, skin color, and hair texture on the experience of being female. Acknowledging and addressing the concepts of power and privilege as they relate to gender, race, and other social identities is critical—it provides the foundation for the work that I do—yet I had not been exposed to these concepts as much as I should have been within my graduate program. As a result, I was not as prepared for how they would play out and affect me in both my professional and personal life.

I had several rude awakenings in the years after graduate school. Now I am grateful for the learning and growth that I experienced as a result, but it wasn't easy at the time. For example, I had to confront my heterosexual privilege. My cousin came out to my family, and I was the last person he told. Given what I do, I was shocked. I thought he would have come out to me first because he knows about all of the diversity work that I do and that I'm open-minded. But that didn't happen. I had to contend with the ways in which I showed up to him from a standpoint of heterosexual privilege. It was a transformative moment for me, because I had to make some decisions about who I was going to be in the world—not only professionally but also personally. So I began this journey to look intentionally at my heterosexual privilege and my religious privilege together and how they intertwined. I intentionally reached out to my LGBTQ colleagues on campus; I did a lot of listening, and I educated myself.

As a result, I developed connections with some great LGBTQ-focused human rights organizations, including Equality Maryland. I also volunteered for a newly created committee called the Marylanders of Color Collective. I hoped to position myself as an ally through this committee and to serve as a bridge between this organization and the people of color in my life who, like me, needed to be challenged on their homophobia. This entailed confronting deeply held religious beliefs among some of my friends and family.

Asked to talk about my experiences with this committee to a broader audience, I agreed to be a guest on *The Marc Steiner Show*, a radio talk show in Baltimore. I then became a founding member of what was then one of the most successful and most visible ally organizations for people of African descent in the nation: the Maryland Black Family Alliance. The Alliance created a video called "Voices of Equality," and I decided to be in it. All of this work came about because of the journey that started with my cousin coming out to other relatives and not to me; it's been a tremendous journey of growth.

While this awakening and others were painful at the time, the knowledge, skills, and self-reflection I've gained from each of them have helped me to do better work and to be a better person. To be able to communicate across cultures and identities, and to interact with and understand people both different from and similar to me is an important life skill. Through my positions in higher education, I have been able to give students both theoretical and real-world perspectives, as well as personal examples of being challenged and expanding my own perspective as a result. I can make the very important point to them that the process of being an open-minded person and a supportive ally while creating inclusive institutions is always a work in progress.

I greatly value the ways in which my professional life informs my personal life. I work hard to be the same person at work and at home. Though I am governed by different rules and language in different spaces, I am still the same person, and I seek to live by the same values. I try to be authentic and seek congruency in my life, a concept that I first learned about in my women's studies classes and WILL. This alignment has had a profound effect on me. I have grown into it because it has come in stages. This is now a gift I can give to my daughter, one that I model for her in an intentional way as much as possible. Being true to myself was one reason I made the decision to confront the problems in my marriage. Though not an easy process, it enabled me to realign my life with my values. My now ex-husband and I are committed to doing the work necessary to create a healthy post-divorce relationship that supports our daughter.

But my transition from being married to single was not seamless. As I spoke my truth without shame and revealed the deep issues within my marriage, my relationships with women in the "married and engaged couple's ministry" at the church my ex-husband and I attended before our breakup ended. I lost many friendships. With the exception of the woman who led the group, everyone else gradually stopped contacting me when my ex-husband and I separated and then divorced. The invitations to dinner and outings slowed to a halt. No one even emailed to ask how I was doing or if I needed anything. It was like my separation and impending divorce was a highly contagious disease for which I needed to be quarantined.

Though that was a hard pill to swallow at the time, I am okay with it now. I have experienced a trimming away of friends who, for whatever reason, could not walk with me through this transformation and transition. The WILL program helped me to find my voice in my personal life, to even know that I had a voice and could use it on my own terms.

I am now experimenting with self-authorship in a number of ways. I'm allowing myself to fail in ways that I didn't allow in the past because I now see failure as part of the process of learning and growth. I am being single in a way that works for me. I have given myself permission to be a different type of single, divorced parent than what I often see around me. I strive to have a personal life and to not define myself only as a parent and a professional. For me, in order to be a professional, a good mom, a good friend, and a good romantic partner, I have to be a good Lisa. I have to love myself first. I have to make time for myself.

Over time, these challenges and transitions have made me a better woman, a better parent, and a better community member. If I had not attended the University of Richmond and completed a program like WILL, I don't know if I would have been able to understand or imagine the possibilities of being my whole self, of embracing all of my intersecting identities and experiences in my personal and professional life. WILL was integral to my development of self-awareness and self-authorship, as well as my sense of social responsibility. It led me to connect with Sister's Circle, Inc., a relationship-based, long-term mentoring program for fifth and sixth grade girls of color, primarily girls of African, African American, and Caribbean descent. I started out as a weekly mentor because I wanted to give back to girls in the community. I had the time, and I knew what it felt like to be in their shoes because of my family's lower-middle-class background and because I had family members who lived at the poverty line. These intersections of class, race, and gender were powerful motivators for me to get involved with this program.

I ended up staying with Sister's Circle as a weekly mentor, working with two mentees annually, for fifteen years. I currently serve as a diversity consultant to the organization. I help train new mentors, and I am a resource person for mentors who have concerns related to cross-cultural communication and interaction. The work I do with Sister's Circle is a powerful and meaningful way to facilitate social change and give back to a community that is in my backyard. Mentors and mentees both have experienced the ripple effects of this work now that many of the girls have gone on to some of the best colleges across the country. Most of these young women would not have accomplished what they have had it not been for the intervention of this program.

People talk about changing lives through certain service organizations, and I know firsthand that this is the case for Sister's Circle, because I've seen it. Being able to enter a young girl's life at a critical moment and guide her as a trusted friend, mentor, and role model so that she sees something beyond her neighborhood is what we provide. We help to broaden young girls' sense of what is possible, because it is hard to be what you can't see.

Just thinking about where I am in my life now really makes me happy! I have been through some challenging life transitions over the years that have helped me become the person I am today. I am now in my forties, and doing my best to live each day being a little more grateful, graceful, loving, and forgiving than the day before. This makes me happy to my core. Chocolate, salsa dancing, hugs, laughing with my family and friends, a fierce new pair of shoes, red wine, and good sleep make me feel pretty darn good, too!

Based on my experiences and where I am today, I would offer this piece of advice to young girls: Do all that you can to discover and listen to your inner voice, then trust it above all other voices. There are too many voices in our world that kill girls and women softly by "should-ing" us to death. Allowing various personal, societal, and institutional forces and voices to determine our destiny and dictate who we should be only helps to fuel the cycle of oppression that is harming our spirits, our bodies, our relationships, and our world. Resisting these destructive forces by owning our power and our voices is essential to creating and sustaining positive social change for women across the globe. Our world needs us as we are meant to be: healthy, whole, and powerful.

CHAPTER 4:

Jennifer

Jennifer Stolarski, class of 1996, decided early on as a WILL* member to pursue a career where she would create better legal and support systems for victims of domestic violence. As she writes, the WILL* program helped "identify how I fit into the world and what I can give back." Currently the Chief Assistant District Attorney in Dekalb County, Georgia, Jennifer continues to develop and implement best practices to address domestic violence. She stresses the importance of meaningful collaboration and always asking who needs to be at the table for any given discussion.

The oldest of four children in a single-parent family, I grew up in a small town in Ohio, the kind of place where everyone knew each other and where there was an unspoken expectation that, once you were grown, you would remain close to home and raise your own family. In many ways, attending the University of Richmond was an unlikely choice for me. Leaving home to attend school in a different state was, at the time, the scariest thing I could imagine doing. But I left the safety and comfort of home and set off to college with the dream of eventually becoming a lawyer.

At the time, I had only a vague sense of what being a lawyer meant. It was the WILL program that gave my dream direction and purpose.

During my first semester in WILL, I took the introductory Women and Sociology course. It was earth shattering. During that course, the professor introduced me to many concepts, and I began to look at things through different lenses and perspectives. The discussions on violence against women, particularly involving intimate partners, resonated with me in profound ways. Although I had not witnessed or experienced this type of violence, I began to see violence in the home as inextricably linked to gender inequality. How could we expect equal pay in the workplace and more women leaders on the national stage if our collective mothers, sisters, and daughters were not safe in their own homes?

WILL balanced academic learning with pragmatic experiences. Building on what I'd learned in the classroom, WILL connected me to a domestic violence safe house where I began to volunteer. For the first time, I realized that the violence itself was perhaps not the worst part of the abuse for the survivors. Rather, it was being displaced from their homes. It was the constant fear of losing their jobs or, worse, their children. It was having to share their very personal experiences over and over again with complete strangers in order to get basic help. It was the prospect of disappointing their families, their faith communities, and their friends, none of whom seemed to understand their reality. It was letting go of the hope that tomorrow would somehow be different and their families would be restored. In short, it was the complete uprooting of their lives that was most challenging.

Seeing violence through the lens of a survivor planted seeds in me that quickly grew into a drive to better understand and address this reality. From that moment, I knew that my legal career would be rooted in helping survivors of violence.

WILL taught me how to approach understanding a problem and the importance of looking at things through perspectives other than my own. I did not realize it at the time, but the deliberate practice of looking through the lens of the survivor would come to define my work. During law school, I purposely participated in a broad spectrum of experiences that would shed light on how the law intersects with the issue of domestic violence.

In addition to developing my professional skills, I learned many other important lessons during those years. So often the legal response to domestic violence is fractured. Multiple courts handle different pieces of what happens to a family. To a survivor, it can feel unnecessarily complicated and confusing. After all, no one experiences violence and thinks that one piece feels like criminal court while another piece feels like civil court. Rather, it just feels like "I need help." This realization stayed with me and continues to inform my work.

When I graduated from law school, I made a deliberate decision to take a position with Georgia Legal Services in Atlanta. During a summer internship with a prosecutor's office, I found personal satisfaction in using my law degree to hold abusers accountable and to protect survivors and their children. But I also saw firsthand how many prosecutors and law enforcement officials were jaded by domestic violence cases. There was frustration with survivors who would recant or who would not show up to testify in court against their abusers. There was a big void between the actual experience of survivors and the prosecutors who handled their criminal cases. So I made an intentional decision to start my legal career by representing survivors in civil cases. At the time, I remember feeling pressure to stick with prosecution because law school culture was so weighted against legal aid work. But ultimately, I chose civil poverty law as my first job because I wanted to cement my understanding of what it feels like to be in the shoes of a survivor. Representing survivors in housing matters, divorce, child custody cases, and public benefits cases would prepare me for what I knew would someday be a shift to prosecution.

In the early days of my career, my physical office was located in Atlanta, but the counties I served were all south of the city, so I would drive an hour or more to meet with clients or go to court. I learned so much during those three years about what real struggle means, including the fact that keeping an appointment at a lawyer's office was often not the highest priority on the long list of issues a survivor had to manage.

I remember a client who stood me up for an appointment where we were supposed to get ready for her temporary protective order hearing. I had driven an hour to meet her in the basement of a church, and she didn't show. When I called her, she wouldn't really give me a good reason for not being there but said she did not want to drop her case. Since I had come all that way, I decided I would just go to her apartment and meet with her. When I got to her place, I saw that she had absolutely no furniture: not a chair, not a bed, not a table. Her abuser had come earlier in the day and taken everything, including her child's medication. She'd missed her appointment with me because she was trying to figure out what to do before her child came home from school. It was an important lesson on the many issues a survivor must juggle.

I also learned how real gaps in systems, like access to legal representation, can impact a survivor's ability to leave an abusive relationship. One of the jurisdictions I served was comprised of four counties. In order to get an emergency *ex parte* temporary protective order, a client had to see a judge in one of these four counties. There was no public transportation between the four counties, so if the presiding judge was not available in the client's home county on the day she needed to get an emergency order, she would either have to wait for a different day or travel to another county. With one particular client, we could not wait for a judge to become available in her home county because of safety issues she and her children faced. She was without transportation, so I picked her up and we traveled to the county where we had been told a judge would be available to see us. However, when we arrived, the judge was no longer available. We then had to travel to a third county to find a judge. It was extremely disheartening. Without transportation or a lawyer to insist on seeing a judge when she kept getting turned away, this victim would not have been able to access a legal remedy that was intended to protect her. How many victims like her have been turned away?

After many hours and many miles, my client finally got her emergency order of protection. I, meanwhile, wasn't just learning how to be a lawyer; I was learning to recognize how the dynamics of the legal system functioned and how to work from *within* a broken system to effect change.

After three years spent directly representing survivors, I moved to prosecuting misdemeanor crimes in the Solicitor-General's Office in DeKalb County, Georgia. I went specifically to a misdemeanor office because, as research shows, the vast majority of domestic violence crimes are charged or resolved as misdemeanors, even when the crimes are actually felonies. I felt like a solicitor's office would give me the best opportunity to immerse myself in prosecuting these types of crimes and to make a difference.

I worked my way up the chain in that office and eventually became Chief of their Domestic Violence Unit. In this role, I oversaw and trained prosecutors in the general trial division to handle domestic violence cases in addition to directly handling those cases that might be at high risk for a future homicide. I attended conferences and seminars on evidence-based prosecution, a prosecutorial approach based on developing the case through evidence like 911 calls, witness statements, medical records, and prior history of police calls as opposed to depending on the victim's testimony to make the case. This approach aligned with my experiences on the civil side; it took the burden away from victims and put the responsibility on the community to hold offenders accountable.

While there I saw many forms of abuse, including abuse inside the courtroom when victims were brave enough to take the stand. For example, one defendant, who presented as polished and charming in the courtroom, was certain that his partner was not going to show up for the trial. When he learned otherwise, he was visibly annoyed. As we waited for the jury to come into the courtroom, he went into the hall and began calling the victim repeatedly, even though he had a "no contact" condition on his bond. This meant that from outside the very courtroom where he was awaiting trial for family violence battery, he was calling and leaving threatening messages to intimidate his victim into not testifying.

This work was quite an education. It was disheartening to hear juries, after acquitting a clear case of abuse, ask afterwards, "Why does she stay?" It is going to take a significant shift for the general public to understand the myriad reasons a woman stays in or returns to an abusive situation, including the fact that she is most at risk for homicide when she leaves.

During this time, I intentionally built relationships with other domestic violence agencies in the community I served. WILL had reinforced my belief in the power of collaboration and had taught me to always start with the question, "Who is missing from this conversation?" WILL taught me the importance of intersections, connections, and collaborations. I built strong relationships with social change organizations that approached the issue of violence against women in innovative and thoughtful ways. I became active in our local domestic violence task force. Because of these relationships, I experienced the power of a coordinated community response to domestic violence.

Law enforcement, prosecution, non-profit organizations, and the community have to work together in intentional and strategic ways if we want to effect change. When I see ideas and initiatives tank, it is often because there is a lack of understanding about who needs to be at the table and how collaborative partnerships work. Because of WILL's training, my work constantly involves conversations about who needs to be part of the decision-making process.

In 2007, I took a hiatus from prosecution and became the director of the Atlanta Volunteer Lawyers Foundation (AVLF)'s Domestic Violence Project. AVLF is a remarkable non-profit that has made a huge impact in Atlanta in terms of getting the legal community to commit to tending to the legal needs of the working poor. Their Domestic Violence Project connects survivors with pro bono attorneys who represent them in civil temporary protective order cases. I was excited by the opportunity to train and engage other attorneys to do the work about which I was so passionate. I was even more excited about increasing survivors' access to legal representation by working to get corporate attorneys at high-powered law firms to step out of their comfort zones and use their law degrees to help victims of domestic violence.

When I became Director of AVLF's Domestic Violence Project in 2007, the project operated out of a very small, shared office space in the Fulton County Courthouse. The physical space presented significant challenges to the integrity and safety of client appointments, which meant that its impact was limited. Because it was a shared space, we often could not have confidential conversations with our clients. Clients did not feel safe disclosing certain information in such a public space. Additionally, our clients' abusers sometimes came to the courthouse looking for them, and we did not have a good space where we could shield them from discovery. Growing the project required fundamentally changing the way we did our work, starting with the location of our office.

During my first two years as Director, I spent much of my time training and mentoring new volunteer lawyers, since stepping into a pro bono domestic violence case can be intimidating for attorneys who do not practice in this area. There are safety and emotional pieces to these cases that most lawyers do not encounter, let alone get any training on, in their usual practices. I believed that if volunteer lawyers felt supported and comfortable while working on their first case, they would return for more cases. I worked tirelessly, therefore, to make sure that every volunteer who took a case through our office had the information and support network necessary to immediately respond if a safety issue arose during the course of representation. That meant pulling in partners from the safe house and from law enforcement to help train and be resources for our volunteers. It also meant being immediately available if any volunteer requested assistance.

I will never forget receiving a call from one of my volunteers who was in a panic because his client was literally circling the city in a car, being chased by her abuser. Because of our established relationship with law enforcement, we immediately got the right people involved to defuse the situation and get the survivor to a place of safety. The volunteer left that experience feeling supported and capable of handling whatever came his way in his next case, and he went on to take many more cases.

I made it a point to personally thank every volunteer at the completion of their case. It was not unusual for them to turn around and thank me for helping them reconnect to why they went to law school in the first place.

I also participated in many community outreach efforts during this time. We had identified a serious problem in Georgia's voter registration requirements, for example, which effectively disenfranchised residents of domestic violence safe houses. I realized that registering to vote required them, under penalty of perjury, to list their physical residence—yet in Georgia, it is a crime to disclose the physical location of a domestic violence safe house. In short, these women could not register to vote without breaking a law, either by committing perjury about the location of their residence or unlawfully disclosing the physical location of the safe house. We used our influence to bring attention to the problem and, as a result, Georgia passed a voter address confidentiality law, which not only creates a safer way for survivors of abuse to exercise their right to vote but also, and more importantly, signifies institutional consideration of a population that is so often invisible.

In 2009, AVLF successfully launched the collaborative Safe Families Office, which offers legal and safety planning assistance to more than three thousand survivors of intimate partner and family violence each year. We also relocated to an unused courtroom and administrative office within the Fulton County Courthouse, increasing our physical space dramatically. Here, survivors can visit the office on a walk-in basis to meet with volunteer lawyers, paralegals, and advocates who offer free legal assistance and safety planning. The work transcends simply filling out legal petitions for protective orders. The office is a survivor-centered partnership between different agencies and offices that focus on holistic and comprehensive services in an effort to meet each client wherever she is in her journey and provide the legal and social services assistance she needs.

At this office, we constantly ask, "What can we do that will make it easier for the survivor to leave this abusive relationship?" Every day of the week, the office sees fifteen to twenty people who get immediate assistance, which gives perspective on the enormity of the problem of domestic violence. For those who come in crisis, needing shelter for themselves and their children, we can immediately and directly assist them.

Our model has gained attention on both the local and national levels. The chief counsel for the American Bar Association Commission on Domestic Violence has described our work at the Safe Families Office as a "model best practices program." But in my time at AVLF the highest praise came from the clients we served. Time and time again, those who had been victimized thanked us for helping them to reclaim their lives, their safety, and their sense of self-worth. While our legal work largely involved the civil temporary protective order process, it's clear that our real work was about empowering survivors.

Toward the end of my tenure at AVLF, our volunteer base had grown by 400 percent and we were placing four times the amount of cases with pro bono attorneys than when I had taken on the project. After so much work and struggle, it felt as though we had hit our stride; our efforts were paying off. So, when I received a call to meet with the newly appointed Solicitor-General for DeKalb County in 2011, I was in no way thinking about the prospect of a new job. But the opportunity to be second in command for one of the largest prosecutorial offices in Georgia was something I could not turn down, though leaving AVLF was one of the hardest decisions I have ever made.

As the Chief Assistant Solicitor-General for DeKalb County, I managed the day-to-day operations of a misdemeanor prosecutor's office with eighty-two employees. I trained prosecutors, law enforcement, judges, and community members about domestic violence on local and state levels. I consulted on legislative issues and shaped policy on how our office handled domestic violence cases and how we educated the general public about domestic violence. For example, we incorporated animal cruelty cases into our Special Victims Unit because of the substantial overlap between domestic violence and animal cruelty.

After six years in the Solicitor-General's Office, I was asked by the newly elected District Attorney to transition with her after her election from the Solicitor-General's Office to the District Attorney's Office. As a Chief Assistant District Attorney, I manage operations for a staff of 190 employees who handle felony crimes. I have the distinct honor of working with attorneys, investigators, and advocates who prosecute domestic violence, sexual assault, crimes against children, elder abuse, and human trafficking cases. I continue to train on a local, state, and national level on issues involving domestic violence, and to work on policy-oriented projects.

As WILL helped shape my career goals, it also forced me to think about my personal relationships. My husband and I met as first-year law students at the University of North Carolina. When we met, I was clear on my career direction and life goals. I knew my career would have a service component and focus on ending violence against women and children. I also knew that I wanted to have children and that I intended to continue working while raising a family. My husband has always respected my work and supported my career choices. He has always earned considerably more than I do in his work as a corporate attorney; however, I have never felt that he values my work any differently.

Parenthood and a career in law is a tough juggling act for men and women alike. When we were expecting our first child, my husband worked as a corporate litigator in a big firm. Although he enjoyed the work and was on the partnership track, he worked very long hours and most weekends. It was not conducive to starting a family, particularly given that I was a full-time lawyer as well. To the surprise of his colleagues, he made the difficult decision to leave the firm and go in-house with a company right before our first child was born. Though it came at a financial price, this career shift allowed him to be more engaged in parenting.

When our first child was born, I was a prosecutor handling jury trials—in fact, I was finishing a jury trial the evening before I went into labor. I had twelve weeks of paid maternity leave. Though I was ready to return to work at the end of my maternity leave, I was not prepared for the crush of balancing parenthood and trial work. Breastfeeding was a particular challenge when I first returned to work. Breaks during trial had to be used to talk to witnesses, do research, and prepare arguments, not to pump breast milk. Also, trial work doesn't promptly or consistently end at 5:00 p.m. so you can leave in time to pick up your child from daycare. The unpredictability was stressful and nothing short of exhausting.

During my time at AVLF, I had two different bosses who taught me important lessons about being a woman in the workplace. The first impressed upon me that you have to ask for what you need—period, and without apology. The second, a man, congratulated me when, after months of worrying about how to broach the topic, I finally worked up the nerve to request a reduced work schedule. He commended me on asking for what I needed and then promptly approved the request.

I worked a reduced schedule of thirty hours per week for a period of time when both my kids were very young. Having one day a week where I did not have to go into the office felt liberating. I could run errands, get things done around the house, volunteer at school, and pick the kids up early. But I also learned that part-time work as a lawyer is very misleading. Although my office hours and paycheck reflected a reduced work schedule, the reality was that I still worked full time, just with more flexible hours. At the time, I was so happy to have the flexibility that the reduced paycheck did not matter. However, I became the lowest-paid attorney on staff even though I continued to work equivalent hours. This is one clear example of the unfinished business of pay equity and work-life balance.

Currently, both my husband and I work full-time schedules. Our children attend public school and after-school programs. Summers are challenging in terms of figuring out childcare. For me, cobbling together the schedule at various camps is one of the hardest parts of being a working-for-pay parent. It's easier when the kids are in school, but it's still a difficult balancing act. During the school year, my husband typically is in charge of getting the kids ready in the mornings, while I am typically in charge of getting the kids home from their after-school programs and taking them to their other activities. Because our children's schools and activities are physically closer to my work than my husband's, transporting kids in the evenings most often falls to me. However, my husband takes on those duties when I have work responsibilities in the evenings. On a typical weeknight, my husband gets home after we have eaten dinner, usually in time to help with the homework. After the kids have gone to bed, we often resume working remotely.

Prior to having children, we had a more consistently equitable division of labor within our home. Now, the demands of parenting in the modern age, the physical proximity of my work to the children, and the flexibility that my job offers have forced us into more traditionally gender-specific roles. I coordinate things related to the children: their appointments, play dates, activities, homework, school projects, and schedules. That is not to say that my husband does not participate. To the contrary, he does an incredible amount for the kids and is very engaged in their lives, with their school functions, and with their extracurricular activities. However, his role is often more task-oriented, whereas my role involves both tasks and management.

There is a different amount of energy and multitasking required to manage a household and children, and unfortunately, it seems like these responsibilities more often fall on the mother's shoulders in a heterosexual partnership, even when both parents work full time. What I see in the lives of my friends who have continued their careers post-children is more and more dependence on outsourcing to cleaning services, food delivery services, and nannies. I have also seen mothers who work for pay drop their careers entirely—not because they were choosing to raise their children as stay-at-home moms but because they could not find a workable balance. Of course, these options are only available to those with the means to pay for services or live on one income. And the pressure only intensifies as the children grow older, perhaps because of the increased demands on kids to be involved in activities. It remains difficult to align the logistics of parenting school-aged children with the demands of a traditional, full-time work schedule.

As is true for the problem of domestic violence, family-life balance won't be solved individual by individual. Systems need to be created, and supported where they already exist, to enable everyone to both actively pursue work for pay and be engaged and present parents.

Looking back on my experience in WILL, I can honestly say that it gave me the tools to analyze the world around me from different perspectives and to ask big questions. WILL helped me to identify my work. And by "work," I do not mean my career, though it is inextricably intertwined in my work; I mean how I fit into the world and what I can give back. WILL taught me that I could effect change. Because of WILL, I learned that I could use my voice to be an agent of change. Unequivocally, WILL pushed me in the direction I was meant to go and equipped me with the tools I needed to make that path my own. I do not know of a more powerful and lasting gift you can give a young woman.

CHAPTER 5:

Sharvari

Sharvari Dalal-Dheini, class of 1997, is an immigration lawyer and first-generation Indian American. Whether through her WILL* internship in Geneva at the World Council on Churches or her service in the Peace Corps in Benin, Sharvari's experiences epitomize what it means to understand, respect, and learn from cultures different from her own. Such cross-cultural understandings have not only been key to her successful career and marriage, but they also have helped to shape and reshape her views about her own life and the lives of women around the world. Most importantly, these insights have amplified her ability to appreciate different perspectives while remaining true to who she is and what she believes.

Looking back on my life thus far, it's clear that it has been shaped by a deep commitment to intercultural understandings, both professionally and personally. Through WILL and all of my work since then, I have learned so many lessons about how women in my own community and in other cultures live and how much they have to teach me, regardless of their education level. I gained so much perspective from WILL's diverse population, especially at a time when our university as a whole had little racial diversity. But it was still striking to me when I arrived in Benin, West Africa, after graduating from the University of Richmond, to live in a community that practiced polygamy. So I'm still constantly thinking and rethinking what I know, or don't know, about women's varied lives around the world.

My interest in intercultural work seems like it has always been with me, probably because I am a first-generation Indian American. My mother's life has inspired me to think a lot about issues related to women and gender. She herself was a pioneer. She moved to the US from India in 1960, and she came by herself. Unable to marry my father in India, she decided she would move to the US on a student visa and establish a life here, and then my father would join her. My mom has always worked outside the home, and she has always encouraged me to take advantage of the opportunities she and my father gave me by coming to this country. Thinking about her life motivated me to think about intersections of gender, race, ethnicity, and nationality even before I could name them as such.

When I arrived at the University of Richmond, I knew that I wanted to make international connections and that I wanted to better understand issues related to gender while connecting with a community of women. I had thought seriously about attending Wellesley College, a women's college; ultimately, however, I decided that the University of Richmond offered the best of both worlds. There, I could be in a co-educational environment while also being a part of a strong community of women by joining WILL.

Not surprisingly, I majored in international studies with minors in women's studies and French. When I studied abroad, I completed my WILL internship in Geneva with the World Council of Churches' refugee division. There, I researched ways to reinterpret persecution as it related to women's basis for seeking asylum. WILL fed my passion for this work.

Through WILL and other campus organizations, I also engaged in local issues. I helped organize a march from campus to the Virginia Capitol to raise awareness about hunger and homelessness, for example. I also did a lot of work with English as a Second Language (ESL) students, both in local schools and with the Richmond Literacy Council.

I knew that after graduation I would continue to increase my understanding of women's lives around the world. Three months after graduating from the University of Richmond, I went to work for the Peace Corps in Benin, West Africa, where I would spend the next few years as a rural community development volunteer. Even for someone who had previously visited under-resourced countries, arriving in Benin as a young American woman was an eye-opening experience. I was stationed in a small town without running water or electricity, eighty kilometers from the nearest paved road. While the national language of Benin was French, most people in my rural town only spoke the local languages. Feeling out of place and out of sorts, I quickly learned that the best way to assimilate myself into the community was to learn from the women of my town. While our lives were vastly different, I learned so much from these women—about myself and about life in general. Recognizing how crucial the roles of these women were to the development of their families and communities, I quickly found my mission in Benin.

While there, I became involved in programs dealing with women and development. In my adopted hometown, I was very involved in local activities like helping to establish a women's group to raise awareness around the importance of women's health, education, and economics. Together with these women, we organized the first, and then the second, International Women's Day celebration. In a town where women were often disregarded, we marched, sang, and danced through the streets, celebrating the lives of women in our community. On a national level, I worked with other Peace Corps volunteers as the vice president of our Women in

Development (WID) program to hold a "take your daughters to work" event where we traveled with girls from their local villages to the larger city to spend a day with women mentors. Many of these girls met a professional woman, touched a computer, and traveled outside of their towns for the first time in their lives. We also established a number of educational scholarships for these girls.

I felt such passion for this work that I extended my stay in Benin for an additional six months. I established a relationship with someone who worked for Benin's Ministry of Women's and Children's Affairs who thought the ministry should do more to get behind the work being done by the Peace Corps volunteers. As a result, I organized a regional gender and development conference with the help of Peace Corps volunteers from other West African nations. We brought mentors in from several neighboring countries, women who worked as weavers, teachers, and small business owners. Girls from these countries came, and we organized workshops and activities that enabled the women to serve as mentors, with a particular emphasis on encouraging girls to continue their education. We were not so concerned that these girls needed an education in order to obtain work or to earn money; our emphasis was on the fact that they needed enough education to be able to read well enough to take care of their families, make informed health decisions (including the ability to read a medical prescription), and successfully complete the many tasks of everyday life.

Our goal was not to enroll every girl in college; instead, we focused on the girls attaining an early elementary school education, with a high school education being a wonderful outcome. To support this work, we had to raise money for scholarships. While the girls did not need much from a US perspective—roughly twenty dollars a year for a uniform and a notebook—many families could not afford it. Also, attending school meant the girls were not home to help with cleaning, cooking, and taking care of their younger siblings, which further depleted their families' resources. We worked on developing scholarships as incentives for families to allow their daughters to attend and remain in school.

The gender inequalities I witnessed in Benin were staggering. I returned home feeling very privileged to be a woman in the US because, though poverty and inequality are far from eradicated stateside, more opportunities are open to me specifically as a middle-class, educated woman. I can not only earn a living but also choose work that allows me some balance in my professional and personal life. My time in Benin helped me better appreciate where I was born, the emphasis my parents placed on education, and the advantages I have as a result.

When I returned to the US, I earned my law degree and a master's in international affairs at American University in Washington, DC. While in law school, I was very involved in the university's human rights clinic and took on pro bono asylum cases in my third year. That work motivated me to do the kind of work that I'm doing today. But not immediately.

When I first got out of law school, I took a job with a private firm in Baltimore to help pay off my law school debt. I eventually transitioned into doing labor and employment law at that firm, but my real passion was immigration. I sought out the one partner who did some immigration work, and I was persistent enough in offering to help out on those cases that he eventually started giving me some of my own. At the same time, my brother, who also worked in immigration law, started sending clients to me. By the end of my time in Baltimore, I primarily focused on immigration work. I also was very engaged with the firm's pro bono committee and helped to start a program with Human Rights First to work on asylum cases. This program became one of the firm's signature pro bono activities, and the Maryland State Bar Association recognized my work with a pro bono award for young lawyers.

After five years, I took a job with the federal government. I knew from the beginning of law school that my goal in life was not to become a partner at a law firm but rather to use my law degree to help create positive social change. While I was able to make a difference in the lives of some of my clients at the firm where I worked, I recognized that the rat race of law firm life and the focus on the firm's bottom line, rather than the law, was not what I wanted for my personal or professional life. While I am always willing to go the extra mile, law firms expect many hours of work not only on cases but on developing business; in order to be successful, the lawyers they employ must spend a lot of time on the clock and away from their families. This makes it even harder to succeed in firm life as a woman. Many of the men I worked with, including the associates, had wives who did not work outside of the home—rarely the case for women with male partners. The men, then, could have families, but still dedicate all of their time to work, billing hours and developing new clients. Most of the women, in contrast, could not devote the same time to this work because they did not have a partner at home taking care of all of the household and childcare work. This became very apparent to me when I had my first child.

Going into private practice was a means to an end toward financial security, but also my way of gaining needed experience. While life in a large law firm is all-consuming, I don't regret for one moment taking the job. It served as an excellent training ground, allowing me to develop litigation expertise, hone client development skills, and learn how to navigate the complex world of immigration through the eyes of my clients. However, the time spent billing and networking became unfulfilling over time, especially as I was expecting my second child and I wanted to ensure that my energy was being channeled toward something I believed in.

So with a toddler, an infant, and my husband by my side, I transitioned into a job with the legal office of a federal agency. My experience in private practice has served me well in my public service work; it has allowed me to climb through the government ranks at a pace that suits my personal needs. My work is primarily focused on employment-based immigration and involves developing policies, drafting regulations, defending the government in litigation, and helping with legislative work. For example, the Obama administration focused on attracting entrepreneurs to invest in start-ups and high-tech companies, so we developed trainings and issued guidelines for the public around best practices to accomplish this goal. Essentially, our agency is responsible for administering immigration benefits. We are not enforcement; we adjudicate and grant immigrant petitions. I typically deal with people who want to come to the US as temporary workers, then get green cards in order to remain in the country, and eventually become United States citizens.

One of the reasons I took a job with the federal government was because of its flexibility. As the mother of two kids, I want a more balanced life—one that allows me to be a mother in the way that I want to be a mother and a professional in the way I want to be a professional. While I am only required to work forty hours a week and I am not required to do extracurricular activities like at the law firm, I often put in many more hours because I want to and can. My office recognizes that this work can be done anywhere at any time, so I can work from home a few days a week and take time off as needed to accommodate my other duties as a mom, wife, volunteer, and coach. My job is interesting and challenging, and it allows for some balance with my personal life.

Law firm life was not about balance, nor was it only about the legal work. I did not like the constant pressure to bill, bill, bill, and I did not appreciate having to constantly worry about whether I had enough clients and billable hours. At my current job, I work hard on issues that I am passionate about, without the pressure of having to stay late to network with people in order to attract new clients. Even in times when the immigration policies of the administration may not be those I agree with and the objectives may sometimes be disheartening, I am thankful to work in a place where I can do meaningful work that allows me to find the balance to be the whole person I want to be.

Right now, I'm finding that happy balance. Even when I have to work long hours, I get home in time to have dinner with my family, attend the kids' soccer games, and help with homework. While I have taken on leadership roles and more responsibility at work, I'm not burned out or frazzled. Rather, I'm working in a way that makes me and the people around me happy. WILL and other life experiences have taught me to think critically about the "superwoman," do-it-all mentality society often expects of women, especially since the US does not have the infrastructure—paid parental leave and affordable childcare, for example—to support it.

Part of what gives me that balance is my marriage. I married a very loving, supportive, and family-oriented man. I think a lot about women's studies issues in my marriage. My husband, Raed, is Lebanese and Muslim; I'm Hindu, born and raised in Maryland; and we live in the United States. I met Raed in Africa while working for the Peace Corps. When we left Africa and decided to move to the US, it was October 2001, one month after 9/11. He had never been to the US before, he barely spoke English, and he was here on a fiancé visa, which meant we had to get married within ninety days for him to be able to stay.

We married within that short time frame, but being in the US was and is difficult, on many different levels, for my husband. As an immigrant, he's had to navigate a new, and often strange, world. After 9/11, being Muslim in America was difficult for all Muslims, but especially difficult for someone who was new to this country and didn't have the support of his own community. Ideologically, it was very hard for him to be in the United States because he grew up during the civil war in Lebanon, when Israel occupied the part of Lebanon where his family lives. So he grew up in a community that has a great deal of animosity toward the US, given its historic support of Israel. His parents were very upset when they found out he had married an American who wasn't Muslim. Before meeting me, they talked of disowning him.

Unfortunately, due to the difficulties of traveling while Raed was in the process of becoming a permanent resident of the United States and I was in the middle of law school, it took a long time for us to overcome these family hurdles. But once we were able to travel to Lebanon to meet his family, these obstacles fell away. When his mother saw the love and respect we had for each other and the respect I had for what was important to his family, I was fully accepted into the family. In the few short weeks we were there, they realized that not all Americans are the same and that I actually shared a lot of their own customs and perspectives. While we cannot always understand each other because of language barriers, we are family. Of course, there are still lively debates in our house as we discuss current events and the differences between the news carried on Arabic satellite channels and the US news media. As a lawyer, I'm usually right in the middle, telling everyone that there are at least two sides to every story!

My husband and I wouldn't be married if he wasn't very progressive, but sometimes I find myself challenging his perspectives on what a woman's role can or should be. He has a very large family—he's one of thirteen—and when we visit his family in Lebanon, I'm reminded that I'm the only woman with a professional job. It's a unique experience for his parents to see that their son's wife is an American lawyer who makes more money than he does; happily, they have grown to respect it.

All the women in Raed's family wear hijab. I question why I should cover my head and whether it's oppressive or not, but in my husband's culture and family, covering is a sign of respect, so I do it when I am with them. I don't mind; I don't care if my head is covered or not, and I don't think wearing a hijab takes anything away from me. It's an interesting discussion to have with his family, because some of my sisters-in-law did not cover before entering this family, either, but they chose to cover after marrying their husbands because of its importance to their father-in-law. As a result, I see that they are respected and have significant control over the family. I think if my husband asked me to cover in the US, I probably wouldn't. In many ways, though, I think it's a braver choice to cover in the US because of how women are singled out for doing so.

One life lesson I learned through WILL is to stay true to myself and to allow my voice to flourish. It's easy to lose sight of the importance of being genuinely oneself, especially within a marriage. In trying to keep up with the harried pace of our family and work life, I have often neglected myself. For someone who is a social and civic-minded being, not spending time with friends or engaging in community work was slowly eating away little pieces of my soul. To not throw a wrench into my family's schedule, I often let things go rather than speak my mind. That often backfired, however, because I would become agitated. These days, when I feel like I might be losing my authenticity and voice, I remind myself that if I'm not being true to myself, I'm also not being true to my husband. And since I have kids, I try to model this important lesson every day.

My husband is an equal partner in my life. He comes from a very different society, one where women do all of the childrearing, cooking, and cleaning, but in our life together, he does most of the cooking and is very involved with the kids. On the days that I work in DC, he's on his own with the kids in the mornings, and often in the evenings as well. We have a good balance between us. But that took time to figure out. We tend to improvise and figure a lot of things out as we go along. When our first child arrived, my husband rearranged his life to be with our son most of the time because I had many additional responsibilities at work and was not home much. The kids strained our relationship in that we no longer had much time for each other. We were exhausted and sleep-deprived. But we are constantly trying to figure it out as new stressors are added to our lives. We make more concerted efforts to take advantage of date nights and to let go of minor things like always having a clean house.

Work is not my top priority now. After having children, I realized that while I like my work and feel it's important, I no longer want to be at the office when it conflicts with time that I could be with my children. Having children has made me a more efficient worker because I have a set time when I leave, and I need to have everything done by that time. I have much more perspective on my work now: it's important, it pays the bills, and I enjoy it, but it's not more important than my kids.

Work is not my husband's priority, either. He used to travel a lot more for his work; now he mainly takes day trips. He also tailors his schedule around the children's since he is typically the one getting them after school and taking them to soccer practice.

When I first returned to the US from the Peace Corps with Raed, our relationship exposed me to issues around Palestinians and the Middle East that were new to me. At that time, we were very active in going to rallies and demonstrations against the Iraq War and in support of Palestinian causes. I cannot be as outspoken on political issues these days due to the nature of my work, however, so my community work now revolves around the kids' education.

Although we are not Christian, we celebrate Christmas. Instead of exchanging gifts with one another, we adopt a family each year and our entire family goes together to deliver their gifts. One year, the family's entire list consisted of groceries. We were able to say to our sons, "Look, they're asking Santa for food: chicken, bread, and other things we take for granted every day." So one of my current causes is getting my kids to be internationally minded and civically engaged, even in small ways, like this example shows. In terms of politics, when we talk about the Middle East, we always differentiate between the state of Israel and people who are Jewish. We make it clear that many people in both Palestine and Israel want peace. When we talk about the current divide amongst Americans, we teach them that generalizations are always dangerous.

My sons are being raised Muslim. That's very important to my husband. My family was never overly religious; part of the way we practice Hinduism, however, is that we believe in one God who can take many different forms. In terms of my children, it doesn't matter to me how they believe or what they call God, as long they believe in a God, behave like God is within people, and respect and help others. So it wouldn't matter to me whether my sons were raised Muslim, Hindu, Christian, or another religion, so long as these values were prioritized. But I do worry that they will be targeted due to their religion given the current anti-Muslim sentiment in the US. This has become even more challenging now, as the most recent election has unfurled a white nationalist sentiment unlike any other that I have witnessed in my lifetime. While we are fortunate that we blend in and live in a very diverse and liberal community in Maryland, we have had to alter some of our practices for fear of being targeted. We stopped sending our kids to Arabic classes after the local mosque was threatened. Even though we are all US citizens, we have frequently experienced being targeted for extra security inspections at airports, faced long waits at secondary inspection when coming home from overseas, and had our livelihoods jeopardized.

These experiences made me question very seriously whether it would be wise for me to attend recent historic protest events, such as the Women's March. In the end, I chose to participate in that march, because as a WILL woman, it was a monumental event for me, but I have chosen not to attend pro-immigration and Muslim rallies, even though those issues are just as near to my heart. Despite our family's service to our community and our nation, our loyalties are often questioned and our actions scrutinized. This has been disheartening for me, as someone who has been a public servant for more than twelve years; for my husband, who chose to become an American citizen; and for my children, who are as American as the next kid.

It is hardest for me to watch my kids struggle with this anti-Muslim sentiment. They have had to learn how to deal with this hatred at a very young age. As they get older and become more critical thinkers, the pain that comes from feeling ostracized is real. As my sons hear fear-mongering news stories about Muslims, we work to teach them that we can't be scared of people's ignorance; instead we must try and teach others by example. One day a few years ago, my son faced a situation in which his classmates said Muslims were bad and should leave the United States. Clearly, these kids did not know what they were saying; they were only repeating sentiments that they had heard at home. My son stood up to them and said, "I'm your friend and I am Muslim. Are you really telling me that you want me to go away?" That conversation ended quickly, and a lesson was learned. I was incredibly proud of my son. The lessons we have imparted to both our boys from early on about the dangers of generalizations and drawing lines have allowed them to stand up to anti-Muslim rhetoric by showing their classmates what it means to be Muslim in America. It is a burden that I wish my boys did not have to shoulder at such a young age, but as we have raised smart, integrated, and passionate young men, I know they will do their part.

Since my time in WILL, and as a result of the many personal and professional experiences I have had, I have rethought what I think a feminist is. In college, I thought feminism meant that women could do what they want and be equal to men. I now think feminism is about women being able to make the choices that are right for their individual situations and women supporting them in those decisions, even if it's not the decision that they have made or would make in the same situation. It's about not being afraid to be yourself. Seeing so many different examples of how women live their lives around the world has made me even more passionate about supporting women in being able to have and make the choices that are best for them. That's an important lesson that I carry with me in my daily life, and one that had its genesis years ago—in college, when I was a women's studies and WILL student.

CHAPTER 6:

Camille

Camille Hammond, class of 1997, is a medical doctor, the CEO of the Tinina Q. Cade Foundation, and the author of The GUUD Book about Infertility. *She says the WILL* program helped her learn "many things that challenged, stretched, and grew my beliefs about power, possibility, and the strength of women." While Camille's story focuses on her personal struggle with infertility, it also shines a light on the broader politics of the body and reproductive health, particularly the financial business that accompanies fertility decisions. She has established the Tinina Q. Cade Foundation to educate and support families about the host of options related to family creation and infertility.*

W hen I was eighteen years old, during the weekend of my college orientation at the University of Richmond, I was rushed to the hospital with severe cramping and bleeding. Following emergency exploratory surgery, I learned that I had severe endometriosis, a condition that would make it very difficult for me to conceive children. I was young and unmarried; at the time, I didn't want to be married. While this news disappointed me, I didn't appreciate the magnitude of that diagnosis then.

Over the next six years, I underwent several rounds of medical treatment and surgery to provide relief from the incapacitating pain I experienced each month during my menses. I believed this surgery would preserve my ability to birth a child when I was ready. Like most young people, I figured that things would just work out. I thought that once I was married, professionally established, financially secure, and ready to conceive, I would do so easily. I truly thought that if I did decide to have a child, I would have an uncomplicated pregnancy, a natural birth, and a seamless transition from great physician and loving wife to super mom.

Life was much more interesting, and a lot harder, than my fantasy.

Here's what actually happened: After graduating from the University of Richmond, I attended the University of Maryland School of Medicine. I married my husband during my third year of medical school. I graduated with honors, and while I pursued a residency in general preventive medicine, we tried to conceive the old-fashioned way. That's when my "pathway to parenthood" fantasy broke under the strain of reality. While I excelled professionally in my residency program at Johns Hopkins and ultimately in my fellowship at the National Institutes of Health, where I focused on fertility preservation for cancer survivors, I was physically and emotionally exhausted—and devastated that I could not conceive—during those years.

Meanwhile, our relatives and acquaintances conceived without difficulty, and some even complained about how easily and often they got pregnant. I wept. I pleaded with God. I ranted to my husband. I raged at my body. Ultimately, my husband and I struggled through five years of infertility, which included countless tears, innumerable prayers, many fertility treatment cycles, financial brokenness, physical hurt, and emotional distress.

After multiple, unsuccessful rounds of very expensive fertility treatment, we were counseled to consider adoption or a gestational carrier to have children. I will forever be grateful that we had insurance to cover a portion of the cost of fertility treatments, and for our doctor, who told us the painful truth—that we needed to stop trying fertility treatments because they were not working, would not work, and that we should save our money. But he didn't say that we couldn't be parents. Instead, he offered another path.

My parents, two of the few people who actually knew about our private struggle, asked if my mom, a fifty-four-year-old, post-menopausal college administrator at the University of Richmond, could carry our baby. We politely declined the invitation. Thankfully, my parents were persistent and had faith that it was possible for her to carry our child, even when my husband and I didn't.

After much discussion, prayer, and months of testing, we moved forward, and my mom became my gestational carrier, which meant that my eggs, fertilized with my husband's sperm, were placed in my mother's uterus. Three of our fertilized embryos were placed into my mother's womb with the hope that one would develop. Much to our surprise, all three embryos thrived. Eight months later, my mom delivered our healthy, perfect triplets. Yes, triplets!

Many of our friends first heard about our infertility, our pregnancy, and the fact that my mother had carried our babies when they saw it on the news. Then some friends—actually, many friends—came forward to privately share that they also struggled with infertility. Ultimately, we were blessed with our miracle babies, albeit in a very non-traditional way.

We received a lot of support throughout this journey. We felt very changed by the experience and wanted to use our experiences to serve and support other families struggling with infertility. It made me reflect on what I learned in WILL about how the personal is political and how these deeply painful, personal struggles, including my own, are often not spoken about in public. Many women and couples confronting infertility feel alone and isolated. My husband

and I ultimately felt the need for transparency—the need to be visible and to say, "You know what? We struggled." I wanted to break the silence in order to bring public attention to the issue of infertility and to provide information about alternative paths to parenthood.

Once we knew that we would be parents, juggling our professional schedules and being present for our children became challenging. I assumed that my husband and I would be able to do the same things we were already doing, which included working more than one hundred collective hours per week. Somehow, we thought we could just add in parenthood and still maintain our intense work schedules.

I was in a medical program that allowed me to take a research rotation when our children were born. This meant that I had to read, write, and publish a paper during my "time off" so I could be home for the first month of my children's lives. And I had the more supportive workplace. My husband was not permitted any leave. We were both residents in training for our medical careers, and the rules that are now in place to better protect residents from excessively long work weeks had not yet been instituted.

A colleague of my husband, another orthopedic resident with children, knew how difficult it was to take time off while being a resident, so he took over for my husband so he could be at our children's birth. We then relied on paid staff to help us once the triplets were born, as we were both working long hours as residents and fellows. Most days, we left for work before the kids were awake and returned home after they had gone to sleep. That said, we felt that the time we did have with our kids was "quality" time, since we lacked the ability to spend the quantity of time with them we wished we could.

About a year after our kids were born, we started the Tinina Q. Cade Foundation, a non-profit organization named in honor of my mother, with the goal of providing other families with the support and love she and my dad had given us to help build our family. We hoped to ultimately provide one $10,000 grant to a family in order to help with the cost of adoption or fertility treatment, and to increase awareness and access to information about overcoming infertility. We worked on the foundation in our very limited free time and, with the support of family and friends, held a fund-raiser to seed the grant.

One day, while sitting with my toddlers, I overheard one of my kids calling our twenty-two-year-old au pair "Mommy," and her responding, "Yes." In my head, I screamed, "Excuse me?"—but I knew kids just speak their truth and call whoever is there for them "Mommy" and "Daddy." I also knew something needed to change immediately.

Since my husband was a surgeon and his potential income far exceeded mine, we decided that I would modify my career plans to allow "us" to be more present with and for our children. Through this process, I learned that there are different ways to contribute to the health and wellness of a household. Money is an important factor, but it's not the only skill or ability that is necessary to a household. In our family, I am the organizer, keeping the house moving and productive as I pay the bills and serve as the point person for all household activities. For our family, the decision for me to come home and for my husband to continue working was a thoughtful, informed decision. This concept of examining personal preferences and strengths while not simply assuming tasks based on pre-designated gender roles was one that I had witnessed while growing up in my parents' home. I had also learned more about gender-based stereotypes and roles, including how to disrupt them, through the WILL program in a more formal capacity. Ultimately, I embraced the opportunity to be at home with my kids. I quit my job, fired our nanny, and began to experience motherhood in a new way.

About six weeks into being home with the kids, I realized that I truly wanted to give back to others experiencing infertility in a more formal role. I learned that being "on" with the kids 24/7 was both fulfilling and exhausting, and I missed consistent interaction with adults. So I decided to run our non-profit, which we had just started the previous year, in a part-time role from our home while caring for our children. We made arrangements for a new childcare provider to help make this work possible.

I believe many of the ideas I learned through WILL about gender equity, women's and men's liberation, the value of time, the importance of relationships, and inter- sections between gender, race, and class have translated into how I view my work, make decisions, and how I parent my children. WILL provided the information; it helped fill in the blanks.

Once our children started school, I committed more time to our organization and ultimately became employed there full time. Initially, I worked without taking a salary, since my husband's salary adequately covered all of our expenses; any money I generated went back into the growth and development of the foundation's infrastructure. This structure was really hard on my ego at first, especially when I talked to friends who had trained right alongside of me and were now making a lot of money practicing medicine. But then I thought, *I'm not making any money, but I'm helping people. Hopefully I'm making some difference in their lives.*

It was actually my husband who helped me alter my perspective. Earlier in our relationship, I had financially sup- ported him. Now he was supporting me, and he never held it over my head that I wasn't bringing in additional income. We were in a partnership, and we were both performing valuable work. We each respected and appreciated what the other was doing. My husband loves and respects the work that I do and, in some ways, feels it is more important than his own. Still, it did take time for me to get my ego in check.

Thanks to our economic situation and our partnership, I had the opportunity to invest time and energy into growing our dream of creating a charity that would support families suffering through infertility. That whisper of a dream has grown with the support of fantastic people and organizations to the point where the Cade Foundation now has an office outside of my home, I earn a salary as the CEO, I employ five staff members, and we have funded more than seventy families to date with up to $10,000 each for adoption and fertility treatments from coast to coast.

Knowing we can't possibly give out enough grants to support everyone who is struggling with infertility, the other goal of the Cade Foundation is to provide families across the country with access to free information about different pathways to parenthood. Information is powerful, and one way we provide information is by utilizing the grant recipients themselves. Each grant recipient is required to give back—to speak their truth and to serve as an ambassador of hope in their communities. The Cade Foundation has a commitment to speaking openly about fertility struggles. We have found that this process of speaking out and information sharing is beneficial to both those speaking and to those listening.

This type of resource sharing not only provides information, but it also instills hope. It increases awareness about fertility options and the politics associated with women's bodies so that families can make informed decisions. Though the decision to adopt or pursue fertility treatment is extremely personal, there are often tremendous sums of money involved, so this very personal experience must also be understood from a political perspective. In my work as the CEO of the Cade Foundation, it is my job to help empower families with information about the different ways in which they may choose to build their families and to help young women in particular understand that women's reproductive health is a highly politically charged and monetized issue.

For example, firms come to college campuses and recruit women to sell their eggs for a significant amount of money, often thousands of dollars. Which women are most likely to respond? As you probably guessed, it is lower-income women—those with fewer resources—who are most likely to respond, as their financial options are limited. Another fraught issue is surrogacy. Often wrongly confused with a gestational carrier (where the egg and sperm come from the couple experiencing infertility), a surrogate is a woman paid to use her own eggs to carry a baby for another couple. Her eggs are removed and fertilized with provided sperm. The embryo is then reinserted into the surrogate's womb. This arrangement, which is illegal in the US, is less expensive than contracting a gestational carrier and is not well regulated. Yet surrogacy is a common practice in the Global South, where women serve as surrogates for comparatively wealthy families in the Global North. The potential for abusing this relationship is frequently ignored or not well understood. This example is one of many that illustrate the importance of being aware of the differing realities of women's lives around the globe and the need to help infertile couples while not exploiting poor women with few economic options.

In short, while the science is clear-cut, the politics are murky. Should women donate genetic material and carry others' babies simply because it is scientifically possible? Should donors be compensated for their genetic material—in other words, should we pay egg and sperm donors? If so, how much is appropriate? Should gestational carriers be paid to carry someone else's baby? What is the value of a "borrowed" womb? The laws regarding these and other reproductive health issues are highly controversial and vary from country to country and state to state. Women need to be aware of the monetized politics associated with their bodies and the bodies of the women "supporting" them, whether it be through egg donation, as a surrogate, or as a gestational carrier, in order to make informed and equitable choices about family building.

These issues are difficult and complex, but the Cade Foundation is committed to helping people understand and navigate them. I now feel blessed by and grateful for my infertility journey, because it was through this experience that I discovered my purpose: to share hope and information about the many pathways to parenthood while helping other families overcome infertility from a fully informed perspective.

CHAPTER 7:

Mary

Mary Mittell, class of 1998, read the feminist healthcare book Our Bodies, Our Selves *as a senior in WILL*, and the power of that text led her to a career in midwifery. Mary tells us how she learned effective activism in WILL* and continues to use those tools in her work today. Her story reveals her deep commitment to cultivating cross-cultural understandings. As a midwife who works with immigrants from around the world, Mary notes how deeply birthing experiences are rooted in one's culture. Her work with pregnant and birthing women has reinforced her conviction that work typically associated with women must be respected, valued, and fairly paid.*

I benefited from mentoring and leadership programs in high school, so I was drawn to the WILL program when I entered college because it encompassed not only structured community and social components but academics as well. I wanted to be in an organization centered on thinking critically about race, gender, and sexual orientation, and WILL met that criteria.

WILL provided a structure and a vehicle for doing political activism. This eased me into activism, making it familiar and achievable. I eventually put my knowledge into practice during my senior year. When a beloved professor at the university was denied tenure, I made an appointment with the provost. I knew it probably wasn't going to change anything, but I had studied alternative methods of political protest, and I wanted to make people feel uncomfortable and slightly guilty about this decision. In my powerlessness, it seemed like my only tool, and I was going to use it. I thought I could plant a seed in the provost's head about the tenure process that might stay with him. As a result of WILL's empowering influence, it didn't even strike me as strange that I would call up the office of one of the university's most powerful leaders, make an appointment, and chat with him about the inadequacies of the tenure process. Because of WILL, I was at a place by the end of my college years where I could create these activist opportunities for myself.

WILL also exposed me to a lot of experiences, conversations, and speakers that I wouldn't have been exposed to otherwise. The program nurtured me as an individual, both in my relationships with the mentors I connected with through the program and in the whole environment the program created. WILL gave me this strong sense that people really cared about what I said, and that I just had to show up and say it. I loved having a whole community of women around me who were thinking about deeply relevant issues. Those conversations might have taken place in small, individual pockets during college anyway, but to have an entire program focused on creating positive social change both in and out of the classroom was amazing. This sense of community among students in WILL intensified and contributed to an already profoundly engaged learning environment.

For example, I remember a fireside chat after a speaker series event where we were talking about issues related to race. Two women, one Black and one Latina, were respectfully arguing—a fascinating moment for me, because it was the first time I had ever experienced a conversation about race where I, as a white person, was completely peripheral to the dialogue. Up until that time, I had always thought about race in a way that centered whiteness; being white was always part of the conversation. This rich discussion challenged my thinking and caught my attention. The safe environment created by WILL allowed for discussions and experiences like that one to happen. The structure and framework the program provided for exploring those complex issues in a safe, supportive space magnified its benefits.

Another profoundly transformative experience for me was reading the book *Our Bodies, Our Selves* as a senior in WILL. The Boston Women's Health Book Collective first published *Our Bodies, Our Selves* in the 1970s as a way to emphasize and promote women taking full ownership of their bodies at a time when less than 10 percent of doctors were women. The book became a widely accessible guide for women who wanted to learn about themselves, have frank discussions with their medical providers, and challenge the male-dominated medical establishment in order to improve health care for women. Since then, *Our Bodies, Our Selves* has been regularly updated and translated into more than thirty languages; it has sold more than 4 million copies worldwide.

Our Bodies, Our Selves is a deeply informative and powerful text. Reading it as a young adult made me want to be a midwife; in fact, when people ask me how or why I decided to be a midwife, my answer always starts with my reading that book as a college senior.

After graduating from college, I did not go directly into a midwifery program. Instead, I moved to El Paso, Texas, where I worked for a year with a Catholic organization that ran a homeless shelter for undocumented immigrants. I often tell people that had I known what I was getting myself into at the time, I might never have gone there. I didn't know much about issues related to undocumented immigrants and the relationship between the US, Mexico, and Central America at the time. My motivation, as a naïve twenty-two-year-old, was finding a job that would allow me to practice my Spanish skills. The organization's guiding philosophy of liberation theology—a Catholic response to poverty and injustice in Latin America that sought to address inequality through targeted political and civic action—also appealed to me.

Emerging from WILL, I saw a lot of potential connections between my beliefs and their organization, particularly around the ways in which gender and race play out in immigration politics, but I don't know that they necessarily saw a lot of connections between their beliefs and mine. For example, the organization was quite conservative on issues related to gender and sexual orientation. Even so, it was such a gift to be able to learn about immigration from immigrants. I met people who had left their homes and risked their lives in order to come to the United States to work and support the families they'd left behind.

One of the major issues the shelter confronted was the School of the Americas, a military program run by the US Department of Defense that trained Central American soldiers. Many of those trainees had been associated with human rights violations in their home countries, so there was concern that the US facilitated these human rights violations. I not only went to protests against the School, but I also organized an event back at the University of Richmond as a recent alum. I had never heard about this organization before beginning my work at the shelter, so I figured others hadn't either. With the help of WILL and my former Spanish professors, I organized a talk about the School in order to raise awareness about this problem—one that I was regularly confronting in El Paso.

Also while in El Paso, I connected with a group of nuns who had started a small family clinic on the outskirts of town, an area surrounded by communities and neighborhoods that did not have running water. When I finished my time at the shelter, I worked at this clinic while finishing the prerequisite courses I needed to attend nursing school. This experience made me rethink what kind of midwife I wanted to be. Until this point, I'd known I wanted to be a midwife, but I'd imagined myself being a midwife to people like me: upper-middle-class white women who came to midwifery because of midwifery's philosophy. Working in that community, however, I saw women, primarily poor and Latina, giving birth in a large county hospital, and it was a rough experience for them. I began to see the role that midwives could play in practicing compassionate healthcare and in advocating for a group that was very disempowered by the healthcare system because they were low-income, Spanish-speaking, and often undocumented. Seeing what they endured played a large role in my decision to move to San Diego and become a nurse-midwife after completing my coursework at Vanderbilt University.

In San Diego, I worked at a community clinic where 95 percent of our patients were Spanish-speaking. I was by far the youngest midwife, but a group of experienced, supportive midwives mentored me and passed on their knowledge. I was nurtured as a new midwife while providing quality care to a population that not only needed it but was also a real joy to work with.

While I did want to leave San Diego eventually—to find a better geographic fit for myself—I ultimately left sooner than I would have because the hospital where we practiced basically ran us off. Most of our patients had public insurance through the state of California, but the hospital wanted to recruit more privately insured patients in order to generate more revenue. As a result, they increasingly limited the number of births we could attend.

Facing this reduction in work, I made a short list of cities that would be a good match for me and applied for jobs in those locations. In the end, I decided to move to Seattle. I liked its environmental consciousness and its neighborhood organization; it felt like a good fit for my personality and my values. Here, I again work at a community clinic, attending births at a small hospital that is very supportive and a great place to practice midwifery. The main difference is that the immigrant population that I work with in Seattle is much more diverse. Our largest groups of clients are Ethiopian, Somali, Vietnamese, and Cambodian. We have Latina clients and a diverse group of white women as well.

Working with such a diverse population is interesting but also very challenging because birth is an event deeply rooted in culture; what women want in a birthing experience is often very different based on their cultural backgrounds. Learning about different cultural beliefs regarding pregnancy and childbirth has been a large part of my education since moving to Seattle.

I absolutely love my work, and I will be a midwife until my bones can't take it anymore. It feels like such a practical and useful way to apply all of my feminist beliefs. I love working with my patients, especially those who are recent immigrants. To me, midwifery is a gift; it provides me with a way to make a very personal, intimate connection with women it would otherwise be very hard to connect with. For example, I have no other overlap in my life where I could form close bonds to people from the Somali community or the Cambodian community. And I can't imagine how I could ever be so welcomed into learning about what their family life is like if I were not their midwife.

But I do, of course, struggle with my work. I am very frustrated with the current state of the US healthcare system—it's deeply flawed—yet I have to work within that system every day. When I think about all of the significant problems in the world, it's easy to feel overwhelmed and dwell on what I am *not* doing. To interrupt this way of thinking, I focus on doing something that I am connected to for whatever reason: because it's my neighborhood, because it's my job, or because it stirs my emotions more than anything else. For me, my main issue is healthcare, especially women's access to healthcare. I do a lot of work within the healthcare community to try to get providers to understand how culture impacts healthcare and, especially, decision-making related to healthcare.

Many of my clients come from Somalia and, like most of us, they generally make decisions related to pregnancy care based on the beliefs and values of their culture. They refuse a lot of care that Americans see as standard or even necessary. I've seen healthcare providers become upset about those decisions because those decisions push their buttons in profound ways. For example, it is very important in the Somali community to avoid a cesarean section at all costs, as well as to avoid any procedure that might increase the chance of needing a cesarean section, like inducing labor. Even in our practice, where we do not do elective inductions and only do them for what we consider legitimate medical reasons, there is still a lot of concern about and resistance to our recommendations. Before I came into this practice, I had never seen a woman more than forty-two weeks pregnant; now, I see it all the time. I have twice seen a baby die in labor because the family declined the repeated recommendations for a cesarean. This, of course, is absolutely traumatizing for everyone involved. It also inevitably results in a lot of questions from the healthcare providers' perspective about why the family did not believe the recommendation or why they would have declined the recommendation.

But it's easy to ask those questions in ways that suggest the asker is not truly looking for answers but simply expressing their own frustration and grief. So I have done a lot of work trying to build better relationships between clients and healthcare providers, to create forums where those questions can be asked and better understood from the families' perspectives. I have had speakers from the Somali community talk to healthcare providers, including midwives at our clinic, about the cultural influences that factor into their decision-making process. It's a challenging community for some of my colleagues to work with, and it can be for me as well, but I'm committed to trying to facilitate better communication

and understanding among and between the Somali community and those of us who serve as their healthcare providers.
My commitment to engaging in these difficult dialogues and
intercultural understandings are a direct result of my time in
the WILL program.

The program also greatly influenced my thinking about
intimate relationships. I remember listening to a WILL
alum speak who mentioned that she would not have been
in the relationship she was in at the time had it not been
for WILL. WILL had shifted her understanding of gender
so profoundly that she found herself with a man she would
not have considered before because he defied conventional
norms of masculinity. It's one of those statements that stuck
with me even though I didn't fully understand it at the time.
Now, I'm married and have a child, and my relationship with
my partner, Guillaume, is characterized by an awareness of
gender roles and a focus on responsibilities being balanced
and fair. We think critically about whether we do things
that align with our gender roles because they are easier and
whether we sometimes need to work harder to break out of
our gender roles. The fact that he's attuned to issues related
to gender is very important to me. When we come home from
parties, he will often comment on who did all of the talking
and who interrupted others. Every time he brings up the gendered dynamics he observes in everyday life, I'm reminded
of my profound love for him, because that understanding is
so important to me as well.

When I met Guillaume, I was reeling from a previous
relationship so I was very no-nonsense about what I needed
from him, and I had very high expectations; I wanted to protect myself from another heartbreaking relationship. From
the beginning, we set our needs on the table. As our relationship has grown and we've become much more intertwined
with one another, we've maintained that same honesty
about communicating our needs and being responsive to
one another. Asking for our needs in a straightforward way

fosters self-awareness and vulnerability in our relationship, and minimizes melodrama. Ours is certainly the healthiest relationship I've ever cultivated.

A few years ago, we had a wedding ceremony with a big party afterwards, but we didn't file any legal paperwork because same-sex marriage was not only illegal but also such an ugly political issue at the time. We didn't feel right taking advantage of our heterosexual privilege by reaping all of the benefits that legalized marriage entails while not everyone had the ability to do so. Right before our daughter, Marion, turned one, the state of Washington legalized same sex-marriage, so we legally married on Marion's first birthday.

It's likely not surprising that I had Marion at home. If I look at my birth experience from my midwife's perspective, I would say, "she had a really easy labor." There were no complications. It was nine hours from the first contraction to the baby being born. It was all just fine and normal. But my lived experience was more like, "that kicked my ass." Going through what amounts to a short and uncomplicated labor was so freaking hard! I would definitely describe labor as painful—incredibly, intensely painful. But it is, at the same time, a really positive memory for me because it's not the contractions that I think of when I think of my daughter's birth; it's what happened along the way.

I had decided that I was going to spend my early labor baking a cake—so when my contractions started, I started baking. I had picked out a time-consuming recipe with many steps because I thought I would need to be distracted. Guillaume puttered around our home getting everything ready as I baked. We ate the cake after Marion was born; when people came to visit, we gave them a slice. And when Marion turned one, we made that same recipe again. That's what I think of when I think of my labor. I was in the comfort and safety of my own home. Midwives were with me, but they were unobtrusive. They were guests in my space rather than the other way around.

Now that I have a child, childcare often feels like an impossible balancing act. Guillaume and I share the responsibility for getting most of the jobs around the house done. We have spent a lot of time figuring out what routine works for our family and how we can divide childcare and home responsibilities in a way that is fair but also pragmatic and functional in our busy lives. We both like to take a step back and look at the big picture about our gender division of labor. I appreciate that Guillaume doesn't just go there because it's important to me but because he wants to examine those divisions through a gendered lens as well.

When we had Marion, I stayed home for four months, and Guillaume spread out his time so that he could work part-time for several months, including after I returned to work. I went through the entire process of trying to figure out maternity leave not understanding how various programs worked together. I remember telling the human resources representative that I simply wanted to know how much time I could get off and when I had to come back to work. If someone had asked me before having Marion whether the US needed better parental leave policies, I would have absolutely said yes, but I would have argued it from a logical headspace, focusing on my knowledge of the vast research that says it makes for healthier babies and must be a public health priority. But now I argue it from the visceral core of my body. I am so angry that there's not a better system. I remember working one random day while on maternity leave because otherwise, I would have temporarily lost my healthcare coverage. The entire system was so unnecessarily cumbersome. While I recognize that Guillaume and I have it better than a lot of other families do, I still am very adamant that what we have is not enough.

When Marion arrived, I was excited about snuggling a little baby; Guillaume, in contrast, was a bit nervous around a tiny baby. It was easy in those early days for him to ask me a lot of questions and defer to me on any aspect related to caring for her. Sometimes it was factual information that I knew the answer to given my education, but often it was a subjective question about whether I thought Marion needed a blanket or wanted to be picked up, questions with no real answers. I made a concerted effort not to answer the questions that I knew I actually did not have the ability to answer. It felt like it would be too easy to tread down this path of me being the expert on Marion and him being my helper.

While we came to parenting with both of us wanting to be co-parents and Guillaume wanting a connected, involved role with Marion, it actually took a lot of intentionality for us to stay true to that path. There were definitely times when it was hard, because as he got more confident taking care of her, he would do things that I would never have done! Whenever this happened, I had to have a conversation in my head: *Is this really important? Should I speak up or should I stay out of it?* Most of the time, I concluded that it was better to stay out of it. Now, I have my routine with Marion and Guillaume has his.

Having a child affected my work in interesting ways. I think there was this presumption that the experience of pregnancy and childbirth would make me a better midwife, but I actually think it made me a worse midwife for a time. Before Marion's birth, it was so clear to me that each woman's experience was her own. When I came back after maternity leave, however, my pregnancy and birth were so in the front of my brain that it was hard for me to push that aside and deal with what the woman in front of me was experiencing, despite knowing that my own pregnancy and childbirth didn't tell me much about hers. There were also practical obstacles. I was pumping when I returned to work. But when you are on call and taking care of someone who is in labor, how do you schedule time to pump? So in instances where I normally would not have stepped out of the room during a labor, I now would whisper to a nurse to ask if she could take care of the laboring mother for thirty minutes while I pumped.

In general, there's just more juggling of tasks and more divided attention now that I'm a parent. I'm also much more resentful when work bleeds into my personal time now, because my personal time seems more precious. It's actually even more precious if it's a day without my daughter, because those days are so rare. I have always believed that people should not have to work every day and that they should not have to take work home all of the time. But it's a much more emotional issue for me now because the stakes are so much higher.

When I first started my current work, I worked full time. I cut back on those hours during my first pregnancy, and when I returned from maternity leave, I started working a 75 percent position rather than full time. While I never thought about this issue prior to having kids, I am now so grateful to work within a healthcare clinic system where it is a completely viable option to work part time and not have it derail my career.

By contrast, Guillaume has had work-related repercussions for having a child. He researches climate change at a university. After Marion's birth, he took time off through the federal government's Family Medical and Leave Act, a policy that allows some workers to take up to twelve weeks of unpaid time off for personal medical reasons, including the birth of a child. When he had almost exhausted his leave time, he went to his boss and said he wanted to continue to work part time. His boss agreed, and as a result, he has very flexible hours and, in many ways, can set his own schedule. That's especially valuable given how unpredictable my schedule can be. But whereas I can work part time and feel like it has no impact on my career trajectory, reducing his hours has definitely impacted Guillaume's career path. Fortunately, he prefers this arrangement and is not necessarily interested in the jobs the next tier up from his; still, it's clear that his decision to work part time has negatively impacted his potential for promotion and perceived status in his workplace.

Work-life balance is my biggest struggle right now. I don't see my friends as much as I'd like. I used to go salsa dancing religiously and now I might get out once a month.

Also, I recently became the manager of my midwifery group. I enjoy stepping outside the day-to-day clinical practice to do larger-scale problem solving and to think strategically about long-term needs and goals for the practice, but that type of work—work that is seemingly never done—bleeds into my free time. There is always work to do, so I inevitably get phone calls and check my work email on my days off. While this administrative work is interesting and important to me, it does not always feel good in terms of my work-life balance. I do a lot of little things for work all of the time, and my to-do list constantly sits in the back of my head. It doesn't feel sustainable, and it doesn't make me happy.

Connected to this lack of balance is the fact that thinking about how to parent takes up a lot of my time and energy. It's a rich, very complicated subject, and there are so many things to say about it. Parents feel so much pressure to try to do what's right, yet it is impossible to figure out what's right when you look at how many decisions you have to make on a daily basis. It's hard to parent, and our culture can make it very isolating. Parents can be very unsupportive and competitive with one another. I find it mind-boggling what people can find to argue about, from sleep-training methods to the proper stroller, instead of supporting each other in how humbling parenting can be and how many amazing life lessons can be learned from a child, especially through mundane, frustrating daily tasks.

My experiences in WILL shaped how I can have these sensitive and fruitful conversations today, whether around cultural conflict between healthcare providers and Somali patients or around parenting strategies that keep me humbled and inspired. WILL didn't tell me about the particulars of these issues, but it taught me how to think critically about issues of gender, race, class, and culture, as well as how to talk about those issues with others in productive ways. It gave me the tools I use daily to think and talk through critically important questions.

CHAPTER 8
Emmanuella

Emmanuella Delva, class of 2002, is a first-generation college student and Haitian American who holds a PhD in biomedical and biological sciences from Emory University. Whether pursuing graduate school or making career choices, her story is one of resiliency. She stayed true to herself, ultimately finding her passion in science policy, where she sees her work positively impact local and global communities. Dedicated to mentoring other minority scientists, she credits WILL* with increasing her self-confidence and helping her to forge her own path.

Anyone who knew me as a middle school kid knows that I first became interested in pursuing a doctoral degree in the sciences when I was in the seventh grade. My first mentor supported my interests and encouraged me to follow my passion, so my story begins with my seventh grade teacher, Mrs. Valerie Thompson. She sensed my interest in science and exposed me to every possible aspect of that world. She made sure that I went on science-related field trips, participated in science fairs, and took every opportunity to conduct experiments. She also encouraged me to pursue science internships and scholarships. Because of her belief in me, I had the confidence to follow my dream throughout high school and college. With her help, I received a full high school science scholarship, and with that came another wonderful mentor, Dr. Harold Afiriyie—who, like Mrs. Thompson, infused confidence in me and helped me solidify my desire to pursue a career in science.

When it came time for college, I made the conscious decision to move away from New York City, the only world I had known for eighteen years, to the University of Richmond in Virginia. My father was not thrilled about this decision, and I feared that leaving home would further fracture our already difficult relationship. We butted heads often. I was a first-generation American growing up in a patriarchal household, and my college decision was the toughest test yet of our relationship. According to my father, education was extremely important, but being close to family was equally important. He thought I could not care for my family while living more than three hundred miles away. I still remember leaving for Richmond as he left for work. He said goodbye to me as if he would see me later that evening when he came home. While I was upset, I held on to the hope that I had made the right decision.

The summer before I started college, I received a brochure in the mail from the WILL program. As I read it, I became more and more excited about starting a new chapter of my life at Richmond. I applied to the WILL program right then and there because I was drawn to the program's emphasis on community building. Having a safe space where I could share my thoughts and feelings about gender and racial dynamics was very important to me. Little did I know how much more the WILL program would influence my life.

Despite my enthusiasm about starting college, I often struggled in my coursework. I quickly realized that most of my classmates had experienced much more adequate college preparation in their high schools than I had. It was frustrating to realize that these students had entered college with more of the skills necessary to excel in the sciences and, more broadly, in college. In addition, I was one of only a handful of African American students in my science classes and I was a first-generation college student. I didn't have a firm sense of what to expect from the college experience, and I felt like an outsider.

Despite these difficulties, I persisted. I did everything I needed to do in order to prepare for graduate school. I did my best, worked hard, took the right courses, pursued summer internships, worked in a laboratory during the school year, and made decent grades. By my senior year, I was applying to graduate school like everyone else. However, unlike most of my classmates, I did not get into a single one of the five graduate programs to which I had applied.

I was completely crushed. It was bad enough having to compete with students much more academically prepared than me; now I also feared that my father might have been right in telling me to stay closer to home for school.

The WILL program was the catalyst for helping me to think critically about the sometimes inhospitable space of science classrooms and to figure out what I wanted to do with my life after Richmond. It wasn't just the women's studies classes that did it for me; it was also the sense of community and family I found within the program. I made some great friends, and have maintained a few of those friendships throughout the years.

My leadership and independence were strengthened through the WILL program. I was somewhat meek when I arrived at Richmond. I kept to myself, and since I was the only minority student in chemistry at the time, it was really hard for me to figure out whether or not science was for me. Through the support of the WILL program, I came to recognize my self-worth. The program helped me become mentally stronger, and it empowered me to figure out my path. I gained the confidence to take on chemistry and to think through a different way to pursue a career in science when I was not initially accepted into graduate school.

I also had a couple of science professors in college, including my research mentor, Dr. Suzanne O'Handley, who instilled in me the confidence to keep working toward my academic dream. With her help and that of my biochemistry professor, Dr. Ellis Bell, I enrolled in a post-baccalaureate program at the Mayo Clinic, which served as a pivotal point in my career. I honed my skills in a breast cancer laboratory while taking, and excelling in, graduate-level courses and reapplying to graduate programs. After one year in this program, 80 percent of the graduate programs I applied to accepted me, and I enrolled in the Biochemistry, Cell, and Developmental Biology (BCDB) program at Emory University.

My time at Emory was often challenging as well. It marked the first time in my academic career when I called my family crying because I didn't think I could succeed. As the only African American student in my entry class, I constantly felt the pressure to perform well, so I looked to students involved in the Black Graduate Student Association (BGSA) for guidance. Over time, I became very involved within both the BGSA and the recruitment committee within the BCDB program. I eventually served as student chair of recruitment for my division and as president of BGSA. In both positions, I worked to ensure that more minority students made it into the application pool and that the administration set a deliberate agenda to ensure that Emory recruited and retained more minority students. I also organized an informal group for students who were already at Emory to connect with incoming students in order to ensure that new students had one person, at the very least, who looked like them with whom they could talk about their experiences. I knew that I would not have made it very far had I not learned the ropes from students who had gone before me. From helping me figure out curricula and qualifying exams to teaching me the best places to eat, upper-class mentors had made a lasting and positive difference in my graduate school experience. I wanted to replicate this practice for every historically underrepresented student at Emory.

I was also extremely fortunate to have a great graduate adviser; I actually think choosing a supportive adviser is just as important, if not more important, than deciding what area of research to pursue. Dr. Andrew Kowalczyk was very approachable: he was willing to listen to me, discuss my experience as a minority student attending a predominantly white institution, and at times debate issues related to the state of race in America. Looking back, I can't imagine completing graduate school without my support group and mentors. Knowing that I was not going through the rough patches alone sustained me. My graduate school friends remain some of my closest friends today because we shared an experience not shared by most, and because we were simply there for one another.

Following graduate school, it hit me that while I had always wanted to pursue a PhD, I had not given much thought to what I would do afterwards. I took a post-doctoral fellowship at St. Jude Children's Research Hospital in Memphis, TN, because, quite honestly, it was a prestigious research opportunity in my field that included gender as a mode of analysis. I studied gender bias in autoimmune disorders and tried to understand why women are more likely than men to develop multiple sclerosis and lupus. While I was there, it became clear to me that I wanted to do something very different with my life; I did not want to work in a laboratory. Though I believed in the research, I realized that I was much happier when working directly with people and using my abilities to make a more direct and immediate impact.

What kept me grounded during this time was my ongoing commitment to mentoring. I sought out the post-doctoral association and again worked with incoming minority postdocs to make sure they had a familiar face to turn to whenever they needed help. I also started pursuing opportunities to teach the general population and young children about science in settings outside of the laboratory. I volunteered at middle schools throughout Memphis and put together a science curriculum to help students learn about making healthy choices in their everyday lives that would lower their risk of getting cancer. This work was very fulfilling because I worked in districts where a significant portion of the students had at least one person in the home who was a heavy smoker. It was great to hear students say, "Oh man, I can't wait to go home and share what I've learned with my parents," in an attempt to stop them from smoking. In addition, most of the students had never met an African American scientist before they met me. Sparking young Black children's interest in science, and modeling that possibility, was deeply gratifying.

Meanwhile, I researched "alternative" science careers and attended seminars to learn about life outside of academia. It was frightening because until that point, all I'd known about was work in academia and in the lab. But as I explored different career options, I soon realized that my real interest might be in science policy. For me, science policy combined the two elements I'd always wanted in my career: science and the ability to work with others to make a positive impact. Once I learned about science policy and its potential to benefit society, I became very interested in it as a career path. I applied and was accepted into the American Association for the Advancement of Science (AAAS) Science and Technology Policy Fellowship program, and I made the move from Memphis to the nation's capital. There, I worked for the United States Agency for International Development (USAID) in the Office of the Senior Coordinator for Gender Equality and Women's Empowerment. I could not have been placed in an agency that aligned more with my interests, given that the agency's sole purpose is to make the world a more equitable place.

I admit that this move was a hard transition. Both my family and I had a hard time grappling with the fact that I had spent six years pursuing a PhD only to pursue a career that didn't involve using my degree directly. We had all thought I would end up working in a research laboratory or teaching cell biology. But I came to realize that while I am not using my knowledge of cell biology in the lab, graduate school taught me many transferable skills that I employ in my current work. For example, I found ways to utilize data to help support USAID's work on gender equality–related topics such as gender-based violence (GBV), child and maternal health, and women's roles in instilling peace and stability in areas of conflict.

It was exciting to use my knowledge and skills in a much different environment. While it took some getting used to, I realized that the tools I'd gained and the skills I'd acquired in graduate school were useful in this line of work. In one instance, I led an effort to inform agency leadership and technical offices about the importance of examining child marriage practices in order to understand how to best address this devastating form of GBV. I used both my communication skills and my data analysis skills to provide talking points that fused anecdotes with hard facts to further gender equity policy and programming. I also worked with others to help develop heat maps in order to show which particular forms of GBV are most prevalent in various regions of the world. It was a very challenging and rewarding two years. It was heartening to be surrounded by amazing people who appreciated my strengths and supported me in discovering my niche in an international development organization, an organization where most scientists do not usually find themselves.

While in DC, I continued working with schools to instill the importance of scientific learning in young minority students. The Baltimore Leadership School for Young Women is an all-girls school that primarily enrolls African American and Latina girls. One year I participated in its annual career symposium, where I talked to middle school students about my life as a scientist turned advocate for a more just society. It was great to see the light in their eyes when I told them what I did. For a few seconds, I felt like a celebrity; the girls were truly amazed to meet a Black female scientist.

My work continues to take me in new, exciting, and challenging directions. I lived in Indonesia for two years, where I assisted USAID in its efforts to build higher education capacity in Indonesia within the areas of science, technology, engineering, and mathematics (STEM). I also led efforts to ensure that all offices and programs would utilize scientific, innovative approaches when implementing programs, and I developed plans to strengthen Indonesia's science and technology ecosystem in collaboration with the country's science academy.

After a two-year tour in Indonesia, I returned to the United States, where I continue to work for USAID in DC. I now work to bring together a diverse set of partners to discover and implement breakthrough solutions in an effort to end extreme poverty by 2030. I work with a great team to help solve global development challenges, such as maternal and child health and food insecurity. I also continue to work on developing strategies for ensuring a prominent presence of women and girls both as beneficiaries of this work and as agents of change within it. While I don't know what the future holds for me, I absolutely love the work that I do because it merges the two loves of my life: science and working toward a more just world. Though this is not where I envisioned my career taking me, I continue to stretch myself and move out of my comfort zone because that is where I am most challenged, learn the most, and am most happy.

If there is anything my life has taught me, it is the importance of being flexible. Career paths are rarely linear. Like me, one may find that a lifelong passion does not easily fit within a clearly defined field of work. Learning to take risks and to challenge myself to get out of my comfort zone has served me well. I have learned that if I don't feel the slightest bit uncomfortable, then I'm likely not doing something worthwhile.

Thinking back on my circuitous educational and career path, I realize that I owe a great deal to the WILL program. While there, I was surrounded by a group of amazing women, both in the faculty and in my fellow students. I was sheltered as a child, so hearing about all of these women's experiences was extremely eye-opening for me. It helped me realize that despite what I might think, I'm not dealing with problems alone, and each of us has that special spark that gives us voice and agency. It was refreshing to be in a space where I felt validated, a space where I felt like there was no judgment. For the first time in my life, I felt comfortable expressing my opinions, and I felt that way because my fellow students and I were very supportive of one another.

Today, from researching gender differences in autoimmune disorders to mentoring young middle school girls to using my scientific knowledge to help decrease gender-based violence, I continue to use my work to address inequality. And I always keep an intentional eye toward mentoring others and serving as a role model for those who will come after me.

CHAPTER 9:
Laura

Laura Haddad, class of 2002, resides in Amman, Jordan, where she works in magazine publishing and raises two children with her German husband. As Laura recounts in her story, the WILL* program helped her learn to keep asking questions and to figure out her own values. Laura gained an intersectional feminist lens in WILL* that continues to guide how she sees the world and acts in it. Professionally, she advocates for magazines to include diverse images of people as well as fluid gender norms. Personally, she ensures that her sons understand the equitable and intentional division of household labor that she and her husband practice.

Children all over the world ask endless "why" and "what if" questions from the time they are able to communicate. Yet we tend to ask fewer and fewer questions as we get older. My participation in the WILL program has encouraged me to take nothing at face value and to keep asking questions. I think I would have buried that aspect of myself without the support I received from WILL.

Growing up in Jordan, where my teachers seemed to look for that one "right answer," I found myself fearful of being wrong, so I stopped entertaining my own ideas. At home, where my protective parents sought to instill our country's cultural norms, which are more collectivist and conformist rather than individualistic, I felt increasingly restrained. My questions were not valued, much less my opinions. Even when I arrived at the University of Richmond in 1998, it seemed as though I was going from one kind of sheltered environment to another as the university, though beautiful and lush compared to the desert backdrop of Jordan, felt isolated and homogenous.

However, when I discovered WILL, I began to break free; I began to ask my own questions again. While a student in WILL, I gradually gained more confidence in using my own voice. This opened up a new world of possibilities for me. WILL was a safe space for me to explore my opinions and values. It connected me to a welcoming and diverse group of women. I felt at ease. WILL was a safe haven for me to aspire to be who I wanted to be, someone not limited or defined by a predetermined set of expectations. I felt included, and I felt heard. I had the right to question myself and others. I learned how to debate respectfully and how to translate ideas into action. I learned there was no single definition of feminism. The program's interdisciplinary academic foundation in women, gender, and sexuality studies freed me intellectually, while the activist component empowered me to lead, challenge, question the status quo, and pursue social change. I learned how to see the world through a gendered lens, a lens that intersects with class, race, nationality, and all other forms of identities. I learned that once you are exposed to a gendered analysis, it stays with you for life. Today it is always there, pushing me to ask questions and think critically about everything.

I soon began to apply what I was learning in WILL to my own experiences. Together, fellow WILL student Candice Renka and I spearheaded an initiative that earned us the University of Richmond's Board of Associates Award for Distinguished Service. Together, we increased awareness of

honor killings in the Middle East from a cross-cultural perspective. Feminists in the US can often be ethnocentric and
monolithic in their approach to addressing issues in other
countries. For example, it's easy for US feminists to con-
demn and be rightly horrified by honor killings in the Middle
East[1] while ignoring or not making the connection between
those tragedies and the high rates of domestic violence and
abuse in the US, where three to four women are killed by
intimate partners every day. Candice and I coauthored an
article that was published in Jordan, brought award-win-
ning Jordanian journalist Rana Husseini to campus to talk
about honor killings, and held awareness-raising sessions that
attracted students, teachers, administrators, and members of
the greater Richmond community.

I continued this sort of work in graduate school at the
University of Michigan, where I earned a master's degree in
modern Middle East and North African studies. I intentionally sought this transnational perspective with my master's,
knowing I eventually wanted to return to Jordan. I loved the
diversity of cultures at the University of Michigan. I started
a Middle East community outreach program with a Jewish
friend. We were fortunate to have students from every country in the Middle East at our school, so we tapped into that
resource and created panels of students to speak in university
classes, local schools, and places of worship about different
topics related to the Middle East. The panel we hosted on the
Israeli and Palestinian conflict was the most popular. We did
not push any one agenda; instead, we tried to expose people
to different views and ideas—for example, by having Israelis
who held very different perspectives from one another on
the same panel.

My education and activism also inform my personal life.
I met Oliver, who is now my spouse, during my first year at the
University of Richmond. I recall discussing with him what
I was learning in WILL about the gender division of labor
in housework and childcare and the equitable distribution of

responsibilities. I'm thankful for those talks because now I find that having an equitable division of household chores is very important to a successful marriage—perhaps even more important than compatible interests, political beliefs, or even equitable income.

Sharing domestic responsibilities comes easily to Oliver. Contrary to how many parents raise their boys, Oliver was raised in Germany by parents who equally shared responsibilities in the home and raised him to be self-sufficient in every way. It is this mindset that we try to bring to our parenting priorities as we raise our two boys, Omar and Shareef. Whereas an Egyptian migrant worker takes out the garbage for all of our neighbors in our apartment building, Omar knows that he's responsible for walking to the outside dumpster to dispose of our rubbish. Whereas other children take for granted that their nanny will attend to their every whim, from putting away their shoes that they have thrown across the living room to getting them a glass of water, our kids are told, "You know where the water cooler is." Our children see both of their parents in the kitchen; they both, from an early age, have been involved in family meal preparations and cleanup, unlike their peers. We know that these early years of seeing gender equality played out at home will be an influencing factor in our sons' future relationships, or so we hope.

Furthermore, despite living in a country where only 16 percent of women participate in the labor force,[2] and where the vast majority of people see my work as merely "passing time" or as a hobby, Omar and Shareef take my paid work seriously, in part because they see that their father values my work and makes it possible for me to carve out the time I need to fulfill my professional responsibilities. They are learning that their father does this not as a favor but as part of his responsibilities as a spouse in an equitable relationship.

As we juggle busy lives full of family, work, and household responsibilities, as well as culturally driven social obligations, it is very easy to forget how privileged our lives are. Just five minutes down the road from our affluent neighborhood in Amman—an increasingly cosmopolitan city where Palestinians, Iraqis, and now Syrians live—is a large community that's poverty-stricken. This community, Jabal Natheef, has a highly dense population comprised primarily of refugees. With political unrest and injustice all around us, we want our children to realize that their perspectives are, in part, shaped by their socioeconomic experience, that our problems and our solutions are interconnected, and that a more equitable distribution of resources is in everyone's best interest.

One area in which we do not experience privilege, and an issue that affects not only my family but also all other Jordanian women married to non-Jordanians, is the way Jordan defines citizenship. As a mother, I cannot pass my Jordanian citizenship to my children. In Jordan, citizenship is passed solely through the father.[3] My two sons, Omar and Shareef, are legally German and US citizens, as I hold dual Jordanian-American citizenship and Oliver has German citizenship. Although my sons were born in Jordan and reside here, they would only be entitled to Jordanian citizenship through a Jordanian father. In 2015, the government started issuing special identification cards for children of Jordanian women married to foreigners. These IDs will help our children obtain driving licenses and benefit from other government services, such as free healthcare and education, and to obtain work permits, own property, and invest in Jordan. However, it does not resolve the larger issue of our children not being treated equally to their peers whose fathers are Jordanian.

Since returning to Jordan, I have applied a lot of what I learned in WILL to my career. I obtained a position working for a women's magazine just as the magazine launched. I learned a great deal there but left after several years, in part because my vision for the magazine differed from that of the publishers. I wanted the magazine to have a social agenda with an emphasis on women's issues, whereas the publishers solely prioritized making money. Also, I was pregnant, and we did not have good childcare options. Most Jordanian women do not work outside of the home and those who do rely on a network of their mothers, sisters, and extended families to help with the children. I didn't have that network, since Oliver's parents live in Germany and my mother and sister live in the US.

I planned to stay home with our son, Omar, for one year and then return to the workforce. Six months later, though, I saw an ad in the paper for a position doing cross-cultural work. Since my father had hired a housekeeper who was willing to take care of Omar for us, I applied and became the senior coordinator of the West Asia–North Africa Forum (now WANA Institute), chaired by Prince Hassan bin Talal. Coordinating this high-profile initiative fit well with my educational background and my deep belief in the importance of cross-cultural understanding. The initiative's goal is to undertake research, host conferences, and conduct training workshops in the areas of social justice, the green economy, and human security by engaging a diverse group of stakeholders in non-politicized and evidence-based discussions around critical development challenges.

In the formidable halls of Majlis El Hassan at the Royal Palace, I was often the only woman present, as well as the only person calling for more participation from women and youth. Before taking this position, I had started to take the benefits of women's representation for granted; now I found myself having to make a case for increased female participation on a local and regional level, which seemed so basic. During my time as senior coordinator, we went from 5 percent female participation to 50 percent. It wasn't difficult to find women willing to become innovators and decision makers from Sudan to Pakistan. Just as WILL showed me how we each have the ability to be leaders in different ways, we brought in unlikely yet powerful change agents who continue to make a difference in unpredictable and often overlooked ways today.

After leaving this position, I returned to magazine publishing. But this time, I found a publishing company whose publisher and managing director operated from a feminist perspective. I became Manager-in-Charge of the only parenting magazine in Jordan, where I make a concerted effort to challenge the notion that family and parenting only concerns women. We include images of fathers as equal partners in parenting, intentionally photographing fathers cooking in the kitchen and reading with their children, for example. We purposely publish images of women, men, and children that have not been photoshopped in order to portray people as they really are, and we include both able-bodied people and people with disabilities. My WILL experience leaves its mark on everything. Without my WILL background, I don't think I would have made a concerted effort to feature female ambassadors to Jordan in their multifaceted roles or to start "Table Talk," roundtable discussions with stakeholders around gender-based issues. From water security to refugees, there isn't a single topic that doesn't directly affect families and require the active participation of both women and men.

Each and every day, I make professional and personal decisions using a gendered lens. The interdisciplinary curriculum in women, gender, and sexuality studies, coupled with WILL's emphasis on applying classroom concepts to our lives and to the world in which we live, taught me to understand issues from a variety of disciplinary standpoints rather than just my own. It taught me the knowledge and skills needed to think in an interdisciplinary way about challenges we are likely to face in our personal and professional lives and as a society. WILL equipped me with the ability to think critically and creatively, to problem solve, and to work as part of a team—skills necessary to thriving and succeeding in any career. I don't take this insight for granted, as I find that most people seem to walk around oblivious to a feminist worldview. I feel good about my work because it's not just about profit; it is about making an important contribution to society by raising awareness about issues not widely covered in the media.

When I first began my current work at Al Marji' Publications, I negotiated a nine-to-five schedule, which worked better for my family than the typical nine-to-six schedule that most workers have in Jordan. Jordanian law stipulates a two-week holiday for workers, which I knew would not work for me, as we have family in both the US and in Germany (Oliver works for the European Union, and they have much better benefits and time off; the EU offers six months of paternity leave for each child and twenty-four days of annual vacation leave), so I negotiated for thirty days off annually. I also negotiated flexibility so that I can attend some of my sons' school functions. Still, I bring a lot of work home, which can be taxing, as I am rarely away from it. And my boss works weekends, holidays, and evenings, which can be tough, as it creates an all-consuming work ethic for me as well.

Since having my youngest son in 2013, I have had the fortune of being able to turn my full-time job into a freelance position that gives me more control over my hours. This has given me the flexibility to fulfill my various responsibilities, as well as achieve the balance in life that I need for my own happiness and that of my family. I used to invest so much of myself—physically, mentally, and emotionally—into my job, with the false notion that my career would satisfy and fulfill my sense of purpose. I depended on it nearly entirely for my self-worth and identity because of the cultural and economic validation I associated with paid work. Work was where I received the most affirmation and felt most valued. I had an incessant need to prove my loyalty and garner approval, even up to a breaking point. I was, in part, duped by the American work ethic that suggests if someone doesn't put in every ounce of effort, or doesn't stay at the office long after the official work day ends, or doesn't take work home, she or he isn't a hard or dedicated worker. Now I appreciate those who place boundaries around their paid work, as I am learning to do now.

There was also a time when I threw myself entirely into my marriage and my children, looking to them to complete me and make me happy. What I have grown to realize is that I'm happiest and the most at peace when I'm in physical, mental, spiritual, and emotional balance, not when I'm casting myself onto any one job or person. Indeed, my spouse, children, and paid work actually end up getting the best of me when I achieve this balance.

I continue to ask difficult questions, which is sometimes met with criticism—like when I published an opinion piece in a Jordanian newspaper that questioned the paternalistic system of oppression that often defines the employer-employee relationship for Jordan's seventy thousand migrant domestic workers. Inspired by an assigned reading from one of my WILL courses, Barbara Ehrenreich's *Nickel and Dimed: On (Not) Getting By in America*, I wrote about how many of my friends and acquaintances who advocate for gender equality or women's rights in Jordan often subjugate the female domestic workers whom they employ. I was shocked by the resistance and outright condemnation my writing generated. Progressive individuals refused to acknowledge the voices that most needed to be heard. If it weren't for my time in WILL, I, too, would be unaware of how unequal power structures oppress and how the oppression of domestic workers is connected to privileges that I and others in my social standing enjoy. WILL has helped me to see beyond my own socioeconomic privilege and apply a critical feminist lens to what I see around me. WILL has helped empower me to continually ask questions and to not let external pressures or my own shortcomings, real or perceived, deter me from speaking my truth, forging my path, and hopefully making a positive difference in the world.

CHAPTER 10:
Jill

Jill Eisenberg, class of 2009, developed a passion for educational equity while teaching in Taiwan on a Fulbright grant and working with Teach for America in the San Francisco Bay Area. The intersectional analysis she learned through WILL* helped her to understand the institutionalized systems that prevent some US children from receiving an adequate education while others thrive. From her impassioned mission to create a library for her low-income third graders to her current work as a senior literary specialist at the largest multicultural children's book publisher in the US, Jill continues to use her own voice to amplify the diverse and often overlooked needs of schoolchildren.

As I sat across the table from Esteban,[1] a third grader, I silently apologized for how little I knew about teaching someone how to read. Teach for America's summer institute had taught me the basics of teaching literacy content, and my school's summer professional development program had taught me behavioral management. Yet as I witnessed Esteban struggling to read a kindergarten picture book, I felt confused about where to begin. Beyond recognizing that he did not know how to access and decode letters, I knew little.

Telling Esteban's family just how far behind he was in school and seeing how betrayed they felt by a school system that had promised to teach him jolted me from a creeping paralysis. I pledged to seek out the best literacy teacher in my school to study under for Esteban's sake, and to never again sit across from another child completely dumbfounded as to where to begin.

Esteban made it to a first grade reading level by the end of our first year together. While his parents and I covered badly needed foundational skills that year, it was not enough for him to move on to fourth grade. One of my most troubling memories is from our last parent-teacher-student conference of the year, a meeting in which Esteban, his mother, his sister, his math teacher, and I had to face the truth that he needed to repeat third grade. As his older sister translated to his mother in Spanish, we discussed how far Esteban had come. His reading level had advanced by a year and a half, and he had grown exponentially in confidence—but it wasn't enough. His math teacher and I laid out what fourth grade would entail and what we could accomplish if we had one more year together in third grade. Although it was his parents' decision to make, we wanted Esteban to own the final decision to stay or move forward, as his success in either grade relied on his buy-in. He ultimately decided to stay.

How could this have happened? Why does it occur to so many children across the United States, one of the most technologically advanced and wealthiest nations in the world? Since that day during my first year serving with Teach for America, I have struggled to understand why so many American children fall prey to our country's educational achievement gap, and what my role is in closing that gap. Although I have tried to make a game-changing difference in the lives of my students as an individual teacher, I know from my coursework and participation in WILL that we can't ignore the interconnections between race, gender, and class and how those identities map onto positions of power, oppression, and inequity. Tackling the larger system is daunting, but I have learned the hard way that individual interventions alone can't fix it. Having recognized just how entrenched the achievement gap is, I feel even more compelled to work to close that gap, both individually and systemically.

WILL helped me that day with Esteban, and it helped me to move forward; it provided me with the language and tools to understand what I faced in my first job, in the adult world, and in society at large. Teaching and its relentless schedule allowed little time to stop, think, and reflect. Yet occasionally I would look up and wonder what happened to other students like Esteban. I remembered the tools and analysis I'd gained in WILL, and I realized that, since leaving college, there was so much I didn't talk about anymore. Once I'd entered the "real world," it had seemed easy to let my college ideas and experiences become fossilized.

I graduated from the University of Richmond in 2009 with a major in history and a double minor in Chinese studies and women, gender, and sexuality studies. I served on the WILL leadership team for two years in college. During my first year in the program, the diversity within WILL captivated me. I focused on soaking in all of the experiences, so much so that I sat in many leadership meetings as a first-year student impatient to get to where many of the women seemed to already be in their thinking about feminist theory.

As a senior member of WILL, I was elected Community Outreach Chair on the leadership team. This position sharpened my leadership skills and empowered me to be the role model and mentor that former WILL members had been for me when I first joined the program. This opportunity gave me confidence in coalition building, as well as a space to address local and national socioeconomic issues that I had studied in women, gender, and sexuality studies classes. Through community outreach, I saw my peers come together to coordinate and collaborate on various social justice issues, such as our work with people experiencing homelessness. True to WILL's mission, these experiences required me to read, think, and take action to bridge theory and practice.

In terms of coursework, I studied race, class, and gender prejudices whose origins predated the founding of the United States, learning how this history still affects twenty-first century society and politics. One summer, I participated in a course taught by Dr. Ooten called "A Course in Motion: The Civil Rights Movement of the South," where my classmates and I traveled in a van across nine southeastern states. This gave me, a regional outsider, an incredible opportunity: exploring and understanding United States history while traveling through and living in the Southeast.

We made our first stop in Prince Edward County, Virginia. Here, we learned about the African American high school students who, in 1951, protested against unequal and inadequate facilities and education. Rather than integrate, the white school board closed the public schools there for five years. Yet, local African American activists persisted in their vision for high-quality education for all children regardless of race or class. As we traveled farther south and deeper into civil rights movement history, I was struck by how much civil rights activism focused on access to education and the physical spaces of schools. In communities throughout the South, African Americans had wanted, and fought for, better education for their children. Yet there I sat in that California classroom with Esteban nearly fifty years after the height of the civil rights movement and wondered what progress the US had actually made in terms of educational access.

One reason my experience with Esteban disheartened me—both on an individual level and, more broadly, within the US education system—was because I had worked in what seemed to be a better, more successful model of public education in Taiwan. After college, I moved to Taiwan to work as a Fulbright Fellow teaching English as a Foreign Language in a low-income coastal township in Yilan county. As an

English Teaching Assistant, I co-taught with a local Taiwanese teacher named Eleanor who was one of the top teachers in the county; she frequently modeled teaching practices to auditoriums filled with local teachers who watched on screen as she taught live in the classroom.

It wasn't until I had my own classroom in the Bay Area during my Teach for America work that I realized how influential and special my year with Eleanor was. We lived on the east coast of Taiwan in an agricultural and fishing county. Eleanor taught me how to work with children—particularly, how to infuse passion into their studies and how to make them feel heard and respected. Together, we taught English as a Foreign Language to 450 students in second through sixth grade. She taught me what it means to be relentless in pursuit of students' academic, social, and emotional development, and together, we created a US culture club for sixth graders and co-wrote an original Readers' Theater script. We practiced reading that script with students for months in preparation for a county-wide competition, and ultimately placed third out of twenty schools in the county; we were the only school in the top ten identified as low-income.

During my time in Taiwan, I was humbled by the entire community's mobilization around education. There, education is truly seen as the key to improving one's life, and the community, including people who have no children in the school system, prioritizes children's educational opportunities. I witnessed one example of this community-wide effort when Eleanor and I organized the town's first neighborhood trick-or-treating event for our school. We enlisted local businesses and government offices to participate in the popular US holiday tradition in order for the Taiwanese students to practice their English skills and experience a piece of US culture. People from the local barbershop, grocery store, police department, and government offices passed out candy to third and fourth graders decked out in costumes, but only if they said "Trick or treat!" in English. Most of the adults did not speak English, and they giggled as much as the students as they asked students to say the English phrase again before giving them candy. This activity allowed the students to be part of the greater community, and it further involved community members as the teachers of their children. An afternoon of trick-or-treating enabled our students to apply their language studies to an authentic English-speaking experience, bolstered their pride in their school and neighborhood, and excited them around the practice of English.

As part of the county's commitment to exposing all students to English language speakers, the Fulbright Fellows participated in a weekly experiential learning activity known as the English Village. The English Village, established by the county as a way to engage Taiwanese students in English language education, was housed in a two-story building with seven rooms filled with pretend stores and offices that one might regularly visit. Each week, a different school's sixth grade class would visit the village as the culmination of their elementary school's English instruction. The students came to practice English in a "real" setting with native English speakers.

This is another example of Yilan county residents' fortitude in providing their children with opportunities to deepen their learning experiences despite the county's lack of financial resources. County residents had raised and allocated taxpayer dollars in order to help fund US Fulbright teachers, yet the number of schools in the county far outstripped the sixteen Americans who taught there—so county residents had to grapple with what to do for the schools that had not gotten an American teacher, despite the fact that all residents had helped pay for one. The English Village was created as a way for every county school student to have the opportunity to interact, however briefly, with US teachers, and served as concrete evidence of the community's devotion to its children and their education.

I left Taiwan very energized to return to the US to work in communities where educational systems were failing to effectively educate students. I drew my energy and commitment from a deep history of grassroots Civil Rights activism, the community engagement work we did in the WILL program, and the energy of the Yilan county residents in Taiwan. But when I compared my work in Teach for America to my work in Taiwan, I was presented with a powerful dichotomy between two distinct educational systems.

I learned over my two years in Teach for America that instead of tackling educational inequities at the national or community level, US schoolteachers and students' parents are too often left to fight alone for their students' success. While the Supreme Court ruling in *Brown v. Board of Education* supposedly racially desegregated US schools over sixty years ago, they are now more segregated than they were before the *Brown* decision. Where I taught in the Bay Area, schools reflect the neighborhoods in which they are located, which is true of most K–12 public schools around the nation. Due to race- and class-based residential segregation, lower-income households are concentrated in specific neighborhoods, and those schools often face a stark lack of resources as a result.

For example, one of the wealthiest suburbs in America buttressed my school's neighborhood. That community raised over $700,000 annually for its public elementary school, a staggering amount that funded art teachers, the school's garden, a computer lab, technology upgrades, and much more. Nearly $100,000 of that money came from one event: an annual crab feed in January. Meanwhile, my public school—located just a few miles away—hosted a movie night and charged one dollar per ticket as a fund-raiser. In order to pay for a spring enrichment week at Yosemite, our fifth graders sold candy bars to their neighbors and siblings, many of whom qualified for food stamps and were in poor health.

Even though my school and the community couldn't raise much money, the parents of my students were just as committed as the parents from the high-achieving, upper-income school next door. Every day, our parents dispelled the stereotype that people from lower-income communities of color are not involved in their children's education. In addition to welcoming me into their homes, families individually volunteered over thirty hours each year at the school. We utilized parents in ways that amplified our educational goals. For example, parents led monthly reading lessons with bilingual texts to show students, many of whom spoke Spanish as their first language, that the study of Spanish is as academically valuable as the study of English, and that critical thinking skills can be practiced in any language.

Shortly before beginning my Teach for America work as an English Language Arts teacher, I learned that the school could not provide any books, much less a classroom library, for my students; it simply wasn't in the budget. If my colleagues and I thought our students needed books, it was up to us to procure them. At first, I thought I could make a library-less literacy class work by using the many printable reading resources available online. Yet as I rifled through a container of Internet-downloaded, poorly stapled paper books, I saw the frustration in my students' eyes. It was the first week of school, and I could not look at my students and continue to try to pass off those drooping, mangled printouts as books.

How could I share the love of reading and invest students in the beauty of illustrations and new stories with staple-bound copier paper? My teaching partner and I began to scrounge for books. We hunted, bargained, and begged. My acquisitions came from library book sales, new and used bookstores, friends, older students, Amazon wish lists, mentors, colleagues, and retiring educators. My kids needed a library, and of all the obstacles they would face on their path towards academic achievement, this one was actually within my control.

As I started to build my library, I was very proud. I developed complex systems for my third graders to check out books: *You can't check out a second book until you return the first one. You have to fill out every piece of information about this* book, including its ISBN, on a check out card. You want to return it? There is a different bin for Jurassic and Triassic dinosaur books. How could you place a Great Depression book back in the Industrial Revolution bin? I sternly controlled the library, as I could not bear for one of the books I had struggled to secure to become damaged or lost.

Predictably, I still had trouble getting my students invested in reading. Despite my beautiful, burgeoning library, I was not giving them enough time to fall in love with the books, to get lost among the shelves, to derive pleasure from the smell of a retired public library book or experience the thrill of hearing the crackling of a new book's spine. I finally saw the problem. I watched a line of seven children in the class library anxiously waiting for a nervous, pencil-wobbling classmate to return his book and fill out the appropriate information for his new selection. The students behind him were getting frantic as the timer ticked down on their independent reading time. My regimented approach to book lending wasn't working; something had to change.

I sought out my literacy mentors and school colleagues, who pointed me toward research and shared their experiences with building successful, healthy classroom libraries, and productive routines. I had to completely alter my system and my thinking. These were not *my* precious books; they were for the students. That was the whole point.

With this new system, the students got "book bags"— large Ziploc bags with their names written in Sharpie on them. They got to take five books home at a time. *You lost it? Okay. You tore it? Whatever. You left it on the playground? I will get you another one. You like the sharks from only the Miocene period? I've got that.*

I realized that staring at book spines does not build a love of reading. I needed to let kids get into them. Yes, the book bins got messed up. Books were lost and torn. Stains, battered covers, and weakening book spines meant they were being opened over and over again. Like strong, callused feet on a student athlete, our classroom library became active and healthy. Yes, it was frustrating that the school budget was small and my classroom budget smaller. Yes, we bought a lot of books with our own money. But bringing high quality, vocabulary-rich, rigorous books to my students was worth using my network as a lever to help my students succeed. Our kids needed real books to explore, not photocopies.

Why had I struggled so much to share the library? Simply put, it was a matter of scarcity. None of us could take for granted the resources we needed to teach children, especially not books. Unlike in Taiwan, where the entire community pitched in, it was the responsibility of individual schools and teachers to acquire what we needed to help our students succeed. My colleagues and I had to coordinate our own book fund-raising and donation efforts. As a result, I solicited books from the nearby, wealthier libraries of the Silicon Valley, and from family friends, to funnel books to my students.

Over the course of two years, I acquired 2,500 books for my classroom. In doing so, I gave my third graders, most of whom were English Language Learners and nearly all of whom qualified for free or reduced lunch, access to a broader range of books and deeper content that fit their diverse interests and reading levels, further facilitating their success in reading.

In my opinion, my teaching experiences in Taiwan and in the Bay Area demonstrate the discrepancies between two very different educational philosophies and systems. Although both schools operate in low-income communities, because education is understood as a communal responsibility in Yilan county, resources are shared there, and all students have access to a solid education. By contrast, in the Bay Area—and across the US—the quality of a child's educational experience is directly related to her or his zip code and dependent upon individual efforts, contributions, and volunteerism. In the US, my fellow teachers and I had to apply for grants, create profiles about why our kids needed classroom material on fund-raising websites, and spend hours scouring book sales, which distracted us from the work of teaching, planning, and building trust within the school community. Our children's educations and chances for success are too often completely dependent upon individual schools' or even individual teachers' abilities to spend inordinate amounts of time securing basic resources like books.

Many people care about education and see it as a path toward achieving a better life. However, the resources of schools should not depend on the wealth or poverty of the surrounding neighborhood or on the whims of donors who may see education as a lifelong commitment or a one-time donation. For example, one anonymous, well-meaning bene-factor donated a $10,000 telescope to my Bay Area school in order for my third graders to study space. Forget that we lived in a light-polluted city—we had no space curric-ulum or astronomy textbooks. This donor wanted to give in a generous and grand way, but at the end of the day, our classrooms needed basic books, construction paper, and cur-riculum material. Only a commitment to a systemic revision of educational funding and resource allocation can ensure that these basic needs are met in every single school, regard-less of the surrounding community's income level.

My experience in Teach for America may not have made me a career teacher, but it did ignite my passion for continu-ing to demand educational equity for all students. While WILL gave me a voice and context for understanding and naming injustice, Teach for America gave me the personal faces to attach to those who suffer the most from unjust pol-icies. I have learned how disparities based on gender, race, and class permeate every industry, policy, and system in the US, and how we need the language of women, gender, and sexuality studies to be able to discuss these issues in terms of power. WILL ensured that I cannot help but think about structures, hierarchies, obvious and subtle forces of power, and what is rendered visible and invisible wherever I am. As a result, I used my time teaching in Taiwan and the Bay Area to examine what was under my direct control, and to begin to understand the larger systems of educational policies.

I began this narrative with a specific example of how this way of thinking has shaped my work and my life. How could my student Esteban make it to third grade without learning how to read? Over the two years I spent teaching Esteban, I dug deeper into this question of why he struggled at school, and I learned that changing the lives of children like him means dismantling the many inequitable policies and systems that work to impair so many students' chances of educational success. Esteban's family had done everything right: His parents had enrolled him in my school because it performed better than the neighboring schools, according to state assessments. They had also secured a place for him at a for-profit, after-school tutoring franchise they could ill afford, a franchise that was good at accepting money, making promises, and boosting high-achieving students' SAT scores but proved dismal at serving young, disadvantaged English Language Learners.

Esteban's story is both unique and completely ordinary. I worked with 120 students during my Teach for America experience, and many had similar or overlapping experiences. Improving their education and future opportunities will require persistent, wholehearted educators, but it will also require a commitment from the *whole* community, beyond the families of students at any one school. It also will require extensive policy reform, particularly around ways in which schools are funded, in order to ensure that students from low-income neighborhoods have access to the basic resources that their counterparts from wealthier neighborhoods have in abundance at their schools.

WILL functioned as an incubator of ideas for me, and it provided me with a safe place to practice dealing with issues I would later face. The relationships I formed because of WILL, and the experiences I had through discussions both in and out of the classroom, equipped me with social change strategies, confidence, a history of effective activism, and a broad definition of leadership that allowed me to begin to see myself as a leader. It gave me the language to articulate what I saw, and it forced me to stop pretending that I wasn't noticing certain unpleasant issues. WILL was one of my most significant college experiences; I came of age as a feminist during my participation in WILL because of its unique offerings, its diverse student body, and its goals to empower participants while bringing awareness to women's contributions to society. Those experiences still inform my work today and help me to continue to act in ways that build a better, more just world.

CHAPTER 11:

Emily

Emily Miller, class of 2010, met a life-changing mentor at a WILL* meeting during her first year in college. Through this relationship and others, she began doing the hard work of reconciling what seemed like two incongruous identities to her at the time: being Catholic and being queer. Her story is one of doing the hard work necessary to live her life authentically. This work eventually led her to earn a master's degree in theological studies at Harvard Divinity School. She now works as Harvard College's Title IX Coordinator.

I was the only girl who played Little League baseball. I loved sports. I attended a Catholic elementary school where I favored the uniform pants to the jumper worn by all of the other girls. I loved being an altar server. I felt deeply connected to my faith. I was sometimes pulled out of class to perform altar server duties for a stranger's funeral. I have four siblings and two of the most loving parents anyone can have. I grew up in a small town in western Pennsylvania where I learned a lot about life from well-meaning, loving people whom I respected, and continue to respect, very much.

It takes a very long time to begin even to entertain the notion that those people may have been wrong, that you may have been misled.

Mine was not an upbringing rife with discord and conflict. I felt loved and supported at every turn. I knew that when I rounded third base, I would see my family and neighbors cheering for me, the little girl with the bowl haircut, who most in attendance probably assumed was a boy.

I remember having questions.

When I was on the track team in ninth grade, I met an eleventh grader who won my heart with his curly hair and his love of the band Dashboard Confessional.

I remember having questions.

In high school, I participated in a youth group led by my friend's parents. During one particular session, we began discussing homosexuality and the Bible. I remember it vividly. We were in the basement of the church. I asked my friend's mom on the side, "Wait, there were gay people in the Bible?" She responded very affirmatively that "homosexual people" were absolutely depicted in the Bible. For some reason, in that moment, I was sure that being gay could not be wrong. My rationale was that if gay people predated the Bible, there was no way that anyone could argue that so many people across time and space could be wrong. This was not, as I am sure you have gathered, the message that our youth group leaders hoped to convey. Rather than internalize the sinfulness of the gay folks, I had identified a community—historical queer people—who shared a struggle that spanned lifetimes.

I remember having questions.

By the time I got to college, I had accumulated many questions. I had a sense that my studies and my experiences there would provide me with answers. I could not have begun to fathom the number of questions yet to come.

In the fall of 2006, I applied to the WILL program. To be honest, I applied because the first friend I made at orientation told me that she thought we should both apply.

Although I felt reluctant to take on too many commitments, especially a program that required a minor, I decided that it would be great for us to get involved in the community together, and I submitted my application by the deadline. As it turned out, my friend never applied. Only slightly peeved, I decided to stick with it, as the process of drafting responses to the application's questions about gender issues, diversity, and leadership had captured my interest. Still, I was slightly wary of the commitment that I had just made.

That same fall, I admitted aloud for the first time that I thought I might be gay. Who was I? I go off to college, join a feminist organization, and become a lesbian? How did I let this happen? I had only been away from home a few months.

Who was I kidding? That little lesbian feminist had been inside of me the entire time.

She was certainly on the baseball team. She was definitely there each morning when I opted for the pants over the jumper. And she was absolutely present in my high school boyfriend's car as I routinely razed any hint of intimacy.

She was just now making her full appearance.

Deep down, she'd known that western Pennsylvania in the 1990s and early 2000s was not a place where she would thrive. Over the course of the next four years, however—in large part because of the WILL program—she found her niche and hit her stride.

To some extent, living an authentic life has always been important to me. From an early age, I knew what I liked and what I did not like. Even when those things were at odds with what folks expected of me as a young girl, I was not terribly worried about it. I attribute this attitude in large part to my parents, because of how they always encouraged me and my siblings to pursue our interests, whatever they might be.

Socially, I think we afford, and continue to afford, significantly more leniency to young girls who undermine society's expectations—girls who embrace hobbies and dress more akin to what we expect for young boys—than we afford to young boys who embrace that which we have traditionally reserved for young girls. This should come as no surprise given that, well, patriarchy exists.

This is all to say that I was absolved of many of my transgressions and written off by most as a "tomboy" throughout my childhood, particularly when I demonstrated any athletic dominance over my male peers. Maybe they thought I would grow out of it. Maybe they thought I would make society's norms my own at some point. Either way, I feel very lucky to have been able to pursue hobbies that captured my interest and don clothing of my choice without much resistance. That is not to say that there were not limits: I begrudgingly sported dresses to most formal functions throughout my adolescence, at my mother's request. Even today, I will wear a dress to some family functions because I know how happy it makes my mother. I have come to realize that I hold a very specific type of privilege in this arena, as I can comfortably dress in both more feminine and masculine ways without feeling any loss of self. I feel very lucky for this flexibility, as I know I would have experienced far more difficulty if I were unable to play up my femininity on occasion. Still, I spent the bulk of my time doing whatever and dressing however I wished as a kid.

Looking back, the primary issue for me growing up was not a lack of authenticity but rather my blindness to the possibilities. I did not see queer people. I did not see grown-ups defying gender conventions. I guess that, deep down, I assumed that I would grow out of it, too.

In fact, I did just the opposite: I grew into it.

Sometimes, out of nowhere, you are given exactly what you never knew you needed. It happened for me during the spring of my first year at the University of Richmond. I desperately needed Chaplain Kate and her guidance, but I never could have told you that because I, myself, had no idea that was what I needed.

After Thanksgiving break that first semester, I came out to a senior friend on the women's club rugby team. Shortly thereafter, I came out to another senior friend on the team. I am forever indebted to those two for taking me under their wings and introducing me to a broader queer community in Richmond. I went home for winter break, and when I returned in January, I kissed a woman for the first time. She went to our neighboring university down the street. The distance, though short, made it feel safer. We only shared that one kiss, but it was really all I needed to confirm what I had long suspected. By February, I started dating my first girlfriend. She was Catholic. I was Catholic. It all seemed to work, and I just willfully repressed any notion that these facets of my identity were at odds.

I thought about quitting Catholicism a few times, but as a mentor I would encounter years later told me, I have found that I am Catholic in the same way that I am a woman. These two identities are very important to me; frankly, quitting Catholicism was never really an option. Before too long, I found that ignoring the perceived conflict between these two identities—my queerness and my Catholicism—was wearing on me. That's when I met Chaplain Kate.

I met her at one of WILL's spring monthly meetings. I debated attending the meeting at all because of the topic. But I went. There, Kate led a conversation about religion, gender, queerness, and spirituality.

After the meeting, I stood around nervously waiting to talk to her. I remember ushering folks ahead of me so that I could speak last, so that we could be alone. When I finally got the chance, I just sort of blurted out something to the effect of: "I am Catholic and gay, and I really want to talk to you." It was a huge moment for me, and Kate was perfect. She invited me to drop by her office hours. A few weeks later, I sat down with her for the first time. I was never the same afterwards.

In the years that followed, Kate walked with me through some of the most challenging identity moments of my life. Each time that I left her office, I felt lighter. Kate helped me to reconcile my faith and my sexual orientation. Without the

WILL program, I probably never would have met her, and I certainly never would have approached her with my questions about faith and sexuality. Where I came from, most of us were conditioned to assume that Catholic folks, particularly those religious enough to commit their lives to ministry, exhibited very conservative sexual politics. In this way, the WILL program provided a sort of consciousness-raising space in which it was possible for a new way of thinking to come to light.

The WILL program is intentional in its programming, pushing people to do this type of identity work. Politics, religion, relationships—nothing is off limits. In the coursework and our discussions, we do not shy away from the "tough stuff." We delve into it. And we are better and stronger for it.

The academic component of the program is critical to this work. It is incredible to share this educational experience with other women and to see the ways in which you and your peers evolve over the course of your four years together. The discussions during the first and second year felt really big. There were issues I had never considered; there were arguments and stances that I had refused to acknowledge as worthwhile. It was a whirlwind experience anchored in Adrienne Rich's notion that we must claim our education. For me, those early years in the WILL program were about opening up to the possibility that I really needed to wrestle with some of what I had been raised to believe—that, in fact, I was doing a disservice to myself in not doing that hard work.

By senior year, the discussions had taken on a whole new tone. We had grown together over the course of four years. We respected one another. We challenged one another. We had more than a few heated debates in which we took much more nuanced stances and held one another accountable for our thought processes and deduced conclusions. Many of us ended up in courses that were not in the women, gender, and sexuality studies (WGSS) program, and we carried our education from WGSS courses into those spaces.

I am not sure that I will ever feel closer to a group of women.

The WILL program is the sum of its parts. The WGSS coursework, the student organization, and the speaker series all work together to enhance a member's experience. You see firsthand how these issues spill over from the classroom into your social life and into the world around you. You realize that these issues are not discrete blocks but rather a tangled web of power and oppression that weaves through every experience. Once you know, you cannot un-know. The WILL program prepares you to embrace this responsibility.

The student organization is a great example of what I'm talking about. Although the students certainly have a voice in crafting the academic piece as well as the speaker series, they have a different level of control over the student organization. The topics covered at the monthly meetings, the types of issues that the students choose to tackle with their activism, and the bonding activities planned for and by members provide great insight into the ever-evolving landscape of the WILL program. The program has structure, but because the makeup of the student leadership changes each year, there is no risk of stagnancy. You can't predict what students will care about during any given year; it has to be organic. Maybe an issue arises on campus. Maybe it's a problem identified in the media. Maybe it's someone's activist interests. Whatever the concern, the student organization is poised to address it. This adaptability keeps the program relevant and its members engaged.

I am wired toward positivity and contentedness. I am oriented toward, "It's fine." But the fact of the matter is that it is not always "fine." There is so much out there that is not "fine," so much beyond my grasp, so much I do not yet know or understand. The WILL program does not tell you this; it shows you. Then it encourages you to act on that knowledge.

My senior year, I finally felt ready to do something about the perceived conflict between my faith and my sexual orientation. Even more, I felt a responsibility to do something.

Chaplain Kate had helped to show me that I could hold both of these identities without sacrificing either. She had helped to heal me. I finally felt ready to turn my attention outward. Because of the growth and awareness that the WILL program facilitated, I felt strong enough to put myself out there and to engage in this work.

Young Emily with the bowl cut did not know what was possible, could not see anyone challenging norms around gender or sexuality. Because of this, I realize just how significant visibility is. I still attend Catholic Mass every week. I love going to Mass. I used to make a concerted effort to dress in more feminine clothes when I attended these services because I did not mind doing so and I preferred not to make anyone around me feel uncomfortable. After realizing how the lack of visibility of queer folks affected my own upbringing, however, I decided that I needed to do my part. Simply put, I needed to be me. Since then, my Mass attire has shifted. I wear outfits that I love, and in which I feel most comfortable. Apart from demonstrating to children in the room that there are alternatives to the norms, I have felt a certain power in demonstrating to other congregants and to the church leadership that I am present. I want the leadership to feel accountable for their words and actions. My hope is that it is more difficult to perpetuate the "sanctity" of our cultural norms when those to whom you are speaking do not all fit the same mold.

I wrote my senior thesis on feminism and the Catholic Church. There was a bit of history: How have feminists, as I defined them, impacted the Church? There were some politics: How does change occur in private institutions? And there was a lot of heart.

During the course of that project, it became even clearer to me that change was never going to come from beyond the walls of the Church. Change had to come from within, from the folks sitting in the pews each weekend. This spilled over and informed my own budding social change strategy on campus.

I was never involved with the queer student groups on campus. I really respected the work that they were doing, but it was just not for me. After my first year, I was openly out at the university, though I did not always wear it on my sleeve. The queer community was relatively small, and my friend group on campus was comprised almost entirely of straight people. I realize now how much being a queer person at the university was like being a queer person at Catholic Mass. You are in the pews (or the classroom, dining hall, or library), you are quietly challenging norms with your dress and romantic relationships, and you are shaking hands and socializing with many folks who are unsure what to make of you at first.

For closeted students at the university, I was a safe person in whom to confide. Being this person was among my most rewarding experiences. Folks in my courses, individuals involved in Greek life, members of athletic teams—there were queer people in every pocket of campus. Knowing first-hand how big of a step it is to tell someone, I was honored to be someone in whom folks felt they could confide.

Every person I encountered taught me so much. The WILL program showed me that, no matter how much you think you know about something, you have to stay open to the reality that you have so much left to learn. An activist's agenda cannot be unbending; it cannot be the type of crusade where you adorn blinders and proceed at whatever cost. People will change you. Experiences will change you. We have no idea what is coming down the line. We have no idea where we will need to turn our attention. We do not know what we do not know.

I had many positive experiences at the university, but there were challenges: deciding if and when to call folks out when they said something homophobic or heteronormative; not feeling a sense of community among queer folks on campus; maintaining the physical and mental energy needed to support closeted queer friends. At the end of the day, the

WILL program provided the sustenance and community that kept me going. Although most members were not queer, I knew that the straight women in the program were true allies to the queer community. One of my favorite memories from a non-WGSS course was when a straight WILL classmate passionately defended queer rights when a non-WILL classmate said something very hurtful. The WILL woman was nearly in tears while challenging the student's stance. It makes all the difference to know that you have folks like that WILL woman by your side.

While writing my senior thesis on feminism and the Catholic Church, I discovered a passion for that line of academic work—a passion that led me to eventually attend Harvard Divinity School (HDS). My area of focus at HDS was women, gender, sexuality, and religion. Many of the faculty at HDS have a background in women's studies. The coursework was not strictly academic in the traditional sense; it involved a good deal of introspection and meditation. Again, I saw how important it is to focus inward before turning my attention outward, before taking my work into the world.

Because of the WILL program, I knew that I needed to find a supportive community in Boston. I also knew that I would need to take intentional steps to make that happen. I emailed the director of the Women's Center to ask if she had any job openings. She didn't at that time, but wanted to meet anyway. A few weeks later, she asked if I would staff the working group on BGLTQ Student Life at Harvard College. Ecstatic, I accepted.

That position provided me with access to folks who provided a network of both personal and professional support. I ended up working as the interim coordinator in the newly established Office of BGLTQ Student Life during my second year at Harvard Divinity School. In a very real way, my queerness and my faith were each a part of nearly every moment of every day over the course of that year. Queer undergraduate students came to talk to me about their faith journeys and struggles. Suddenly, though I will never share Chaplain Kate's pastoral gifts, I found myself sitting on the other side of the table, listening to folks talk about their concerns and their challenges.

When I told people that I was at HDS and working in the BGLTQ office, I would generally find myself faced with a barrage of questions about how I made that work. At some point, I had forgotten that it had ever not worked.

Change can come down like a landslide.

I try to infuse my work with an appreciation for interpersonal connections. I want people to understand the invaluable contribution that such relationships can make to a life. I want people to see that we are simultaneously alike and different and that our differences, far from dividing us, can really make us a stronger whole. When I was working in the BGLTQ office, several students approached me about holding a speed dating event for women and trans-identified folks. We decided to invite individuals at neighboring colleges and universities to participate. When I told some of my colleagues about the event, they chuckled. *Speed dating?* When more than a hundred women and trans-identified people from eleven local colleges and universities attended, their chuckles subsided. People were starving for interpersonal connections.

We also held programs for folks about being "Out at Work" and being "Out Abroad." I wanted folks to realize that there is no need to reinvent the wheel. Others have come before us and others will come after us. These programs provided a space for folks to share their experiences and to inquire about whatever was on their mind. The questions ranged from safety concerns to "Where is *the place* to party?" I do not think that either of these topics is more pressing or important than the other.

Others have come before us, and others will come after us. For decades, the WILL program has been creating spaces for young women, transgender, and gender-nonconforming students to come together to delve into difficult issues, claim their educations, figure out what sparks their interest, and decide what they are going to do with the responsibility that this education places on their shoulders.

Through the WILL program, I found answers to some of my questions, but for the most part I found that my questions begged more questions. More important, I found a community of people who were asking questions that interested me and were interested in my questions. The WILL model demonstrates the necessity of permeable boundaries between the individual, the immediate community, and the global community when grappling with some of life's biggest, toughest questions.

I try every day to approach the world purposefully, openly, and with understanding. I see great value in the range of experiences I have had. I feel grateful to have been born to parents who allowed me to pursue my passions, even when that meant undermining society's expectations. I feel grateful to have experienced the WILL program. Though formally enrolled for four short years, I have found that the program's reach and impact have extended well beyond those years.

I remember having questions. I remember wanting answers. I remember finding WILL. Sometimes, out of nowhere, you are given exactly that which you never knew you needed.

CHAPTER 12:
Jah

Jah Akande, class of 2013, has been an activist since the age of fifteen, when he first lobbied legislators at Virginia's General Assembly. As a high school student, he became the first Black student and the first out LGBTQ student to serve as student body president. In college, he organized buses of students to lobby on behalf of LGBTQ rights, and he continues that commitment to human rights advocacy today while attending the University of Virginia School of Law. Jah credits the WILL* program for being a safe and supportive space as he transitioned to living his true gender identity as male. Although Jah's story emphasizes his activism, it's also a very personal one about authenticity.

Activism saved my life.

It all started in the tenth grade. I had been outed as lesbian the year before, and I was grappling with my identity while reconciling the implications of what this would mean for my relationship with my family, my religion, and my broader community. It wasn't a good time for me. I felt suicidal. I didn't want to be attracted to girls, but a force was inside of me that I could not shake. To make matters more complicated, and to the immense disappointment of those around me, my tomboy persona did not recede as I grew older.

Much later, I came to understand that this was *my* persona, and that my gender identity simply did not match the gender I had been assigned at birth. In short, my gender identity was male. All of this tension, along with my own self-hatred and difficult relationship with my father at the time, pushed me to the edge.[1]

I lived the two most difficult years of my life when I was thirteen and fourteen. I am the eldest of five children; I was one of four girls and we had a younger baby brother, a fact that delighted my parents. I didn't seem to fit; I never did. I was the kid who everyone knew was different, but no one in the family talked about it, at least not to my face. After I was outed, it was as if the elephant in the room had become visible.

I adopted a lesbian identity because lesbian was what people called me. "Gay" was the term my family and friends used to describe my behavior; a different gender identity was not a possibility that I or anyone else considered at the time. Many loved ones around me prayed that it was a phase. Sadly, I did, too. I wasn't interested in creating confusion or confrontation.

In middle school, I was the hard-working, clever, sporty kid who took political positions. I worked diligently and persevered to get into a very competitive leadership program at my high school. There, I was one of four Black students among 160 peers. The students in this program were also very economically privileged; this directly contrasted with my predominantly working-class upbringing. Because of my different background and because being lesbian was such a stigma, I feared that I would ruin my reputation, my family's reputation, or the reputation of my community by being out.

As a result, the start of high school was hard. I fought against my family and my own self as I tried to find my way. I didn't know who I was. During my most distant and darkest moments in high school, a history teacher reached out to me and encouraged me to join ROSMY, the Richmond Organization for Sexual Minority Youth (now known as Side by Side). I found a place where I belonged within the first five minutes of my first meeting there. I met other gender-non-conforming, lesbian, and gay young people. I finally felt like I wasn't alone. It was such a welcome contrast to middle school and high school, where I had not encountered one visible gender-nonconforming person in eight years.

At the end of my first ROSMY meeting, I was invited to apply for their youth leadership program, which would hone both my public speaking and organizational skills while exposing me to LGBTQ businesspeople, allies, and role models in the community. Through ROSMY, I helped organize the first LGBTQ prom in Virginia. Celebrating people like me with people like me was overwhelmingly positive and affirming. It was at this point in my life that I felt I was truly loved, appreciated, and accepted.

With this increased confidence, I began organizing youth in my local school district to lobby the Virginia General Assembly for workplace non-discrimination policies. I can still remember the first weekend that I lobbied. I was fifteen years old. It was such a positive experience to be actively working for social change. Upon returning to school that Monday, I took a leadership role in my school's gay–straight alliance. With the help of ROSMY's public speaking workshops, I started to become more comfortable speaking up in heteronormative spaces, which eventually gave me the confidence to hold other leadership roles in high school. During my senior year, I was elected president of Douglas Freeman High School itself. I became the first person of color and the first out LGBTQ person to serve as the school's student government president.

When I reflect on my experiences in high school today, I am thankful for them, because they molded me into the person I am today. I have become stronger in my beliefs and dedication to uplifting marginalized communities. I am blessed to have found, at a young age, my passion for the LGBTQ community, activism, and the radical love and support to be myself. It was as a result of this radical love that I recognized—albeit a few years later, at age nineteen—that I am in fact a transgender male rather than a lesbian. In the years since, I have educated myself about who I've always been and have truly sought to own and understand the multifaceted identities I experienced growing up, first as a Black lesbian activist and now as a Black transgender male activist. Even now that I am married to a woman, have undergone hormone therapy, and live every day of my life as the man I always was, I will *always* consider myself queer, as the experience of coming out as lesbian is so integrated into my life.

After graduating from high school, I attended college at the University of Richmond. I was reluctant to do so at first. It was just as white and heteronormative as my high school; in fact, they are only three miles away from each other. But this private liberal arts college had so much to offer, including the fact that it fully funded my education through an academic scholarship.

Upon arriving at the university, I found that undergraduates were divided into two separate residential colleges, one for men and one for women—a system I didn't fit into. I remember not attending the induction to the women's college, Westhampton College, because it did not feel right.[2]

But as a seventeen-year old radical LGBTQ activist, I immediately gravitated to WILL, which is situated within Westhampton College. WILL members were the first to reach out to me and acknowledge my confusion and discomfort with the "Westhampton" classification. So, without hesitation, I applied and joined WILL my first semester. It turned out to be a powerful program that aligned with my ideals of social change, community, education, and elevation of the marginalized. I believed that WILL would be a safe space—a place where I would not be labeled and where I would have the opportunity to live amongst other activists and learn about feminism, a movement that would have a profound impact on my life. I was not disappointed.

I used my organizing skills to help galvanize students in WILL and other organizations to support LGBTQ activism in Richmond. Though the university had tremendous resources and progressive faculty, I was frustrated to find a fairly complacent student body when I arrived. Many students were content living within the bubble of campus. When I approached them about building momentum in the LGBTQ movement in Virginia, they replied that it was "a lost cause" given Virginia's conservative politics. They did not believe LGBTQ-friendly policies were a possibility. But I didn't give up. With the help of my friends in WILL, friends from high school, allies at the university, and work colleagues, I grew the lobbying population at the university from six students into a group of forty. I catalyzed the movement that I had always imagined was possible.

For that, I am thankful. WILL was good for me and good to me. WILL became the home that ROSMY had been for me when I was younger. I received the love, support, and patience to truly understand myself and my masculinity.

We regularly volunteered in the Richmond community. In one of my required women, gender, and sexuality studies classes, for example, I worked on ROSMY's LGBTQ prom for my action project, and the entire class got involved. Everyone helped out, and that year's alternative prom was the largest one ever, reaching more than one hundred teenagers across Virginia. Through WILL, I made lifelong connections with women who were just as passionate as I was about doing social justice work. My friends in WILL understood the intersections of race, gender, sexuality, and poverty, and the importance of translating that understanding into advocacy.

Through WILL, I also obtained a transformative internship. I interned with Equality Virginia, Virginia's non-partisan LGBTQ advocacy organization, organizing for LGBTQ legislation within Virginia's General Assembly. My position involved working specifically with the Black Caucus to build a relationship between the Caucus and Equality Virginia, whose staff was all white at the time and not well connected within the Black community. This work was right up my alley, and it paved the way for my other political internships and expanded my network considerably. I traveled all over the state to meet with Delegates and Senators as a Black youth advocating for the recognition of LGBTQ rights by Black community leaders, and I gained a lot of support for LGBTQ legislation as a result of those conversations. Many representatives who I spoke with had never before, to their knowledge, met an LGBTQ person of color. They knew that the lack of rights for the LGBTQ community was a problem, but the lack of rights did not affect them personally, so they abstained from supporting LGBTQ legislation most of the time. Some of them shifted their perspective after talking with me, which reinforced my dedication to this work.

WILL also prepared me for my journey to London when I was nineteen. I found studying abroad in a new community freeing, and it enabled me to finally self-identify as male. London is fairly open to transgender identities; in fact, transgender rights are incorporated into human rights legislation for the entire country. Living there helped me imagine and live my truth.

Within a few months of returning to the University of Richmond and with the support of my friends and professors, including the WILL directors, I had the courage to ask people to start calling me "he," despite the fact that I would not physically transition until after graduation. I even changed colleges—from Westhampton to Richmond College, the men's college—to align with my gender identity. WILL supported me in this transition, making it clear that as a man, I could still be involved. It was almost second nature, as WILL had drilled into me that I could be myself and that authenticity would become the source of my own liberation. Soon after, WILL formally opened the program to women, gender non-conforming, and transgender students, and added an asterisk to its name, WILL*, to indicate this fact.

Upon returning from London, I worked hard as president and cofounder of the Black Alliance for Sexual Minority Equality (BASE). In this role, I reached out to students who felt they didn't have a voice in the mostly white LGBTQ activist group on campus. BASE formed strong connections across campus to better discuss and understand the intersections of race and LBGTQ issues. Through my work in WILL, BASE, and other organizations, I hoped to build a legacy that would last long after I graduated.

I also interned with Delegate Joe Morrissey in the Virginia House of Representatives during this time. It was incredibly rewarding work. I helped to advance Delegate Morrissey's support of lesbian, gay, bisexual, and, eventually, transgender rights. He became one of the first delegates to sign the workplace LGBTQ non-discrimination clause. He was passionate, engaged in the community, and a fighter. He helped make me feel comfortable in Virginia politics as a transgender man. He was extremely supportive when introducing me to lobbyists and fellow lawmakers; he always eased any awkwardness by addressing me as "Jah" instead of "Jamaica," which was particularly significant because he first met me when I was a fifteen-year-old girl named Jamaica lobbying for ROSMY. His support was empowering, especially in the very conservative environment of the Virginia legislature.

While interning in the Virginia House of Delegates, I continued my work with Equality Virginia, pushing to gain support for a statewide non-discrimination employment bill that included LGBTQ people. Unfortunately, Governor McDonnell had just rescinded an executive order that protected LGBTQ individuals who worked for the state of Virginia. Joe Morrissey supported me in speaking publically to both the House and Senate in support of the bill as a transgender Virginian. The bill didn't pass, but it got farther along in the deliberation process than ever before. That experience was by far the most visible I had ever been as a transgender activist, and it led me to become committed to trans visibility. So many trans people are, understandably, afraid to come out because we are treated differently and are at risk of not being hired or being fired on the basis of our identity. But the loneliness and isolation I experienced as a teen when I had no models of people like me drives me to be a visible advocate today.

Virginia is changing: it is more moderate today, and LGBTQ rights have increased, thanks to progress at the federal level. But LGBTQ rights are something Virginians must continue to work on as a state. So much has changed since I was fifteen. As I write this today, same-sex couples have the freedom to marry in Virginia and now, with the 2015 Supreme Court decision, it's the law of the land! Dozens of large businesses in the state have adopted pro-LGBTQ policies in order to create a safe and progressive work environment. As of 2016, we have LGBTQ advocates in the state's highest office of governor. I am proud to have been a small factor in changing Virginia's political landscape. But there is still much work to be done.

In terms of my personal life, three weeks after graduating from college, I moved to London in order to marry my girlfriend and take a position with Teach First, the British equivalent of Teach for America. I applied for the job as a male applicant and explained during the interview process that I was transgender. They completely accepted me, and this was before I started hormone therapy. I taught English in an inner-city school where my students called me Mr. Jamaica Akande or Mr. Jah Akande. The staff at Teach First acknowledged my male identity before I started testosterone. That kind of acceptance matters. After living and working in England for seven months, I started testosterone therapy, which is covered by National Health Services in England. Since then, I have seen an even larger transformation in my confidence.

Now that I am experiencing life as male rather than as a lesbian woman, I feel freer and more comfortable with myself. I am almost never misgendered, and I feel safer when I am out in the world, though not necessarily in the United States as a Black male. However, at times I look around and grasp that it is almost as though I am passing. My activism is still inherent, but I don't "wear it" on my body any longer. This idea for me is conflicting. My noticeable visibility as an LGBTQ person has ended, and I have found myself having to navigate safe and familiar spaces cognizant of both my male and heterosexual privilege. I recognize the privilege that I now have in society. I am safer walking the streets alone at night. I am able to make connections at work through my male privilege. While teaching in London, my students responded to me at times with less resistance than they did to my female colleagues as a result of my gender. With this privilege comes great responsibility, and I integrate my awareness of that fact into my intersectional approach to teaching and building relationships. I am always encouraging discussion and debate around uncomfortable issues of sexism, racism, homophobia, transphobia, and classism. That is who I was before, of course; now I am just more aware of my own need to be accountable and steadfast in this sort of leadership.

I took a step back from political activism as I built my new married life and adjusted to the ins and outs of teaching in a tough urban setting. I tried to find moments in my classroom where I could incorporate my principles of social change. I tried hard to be a role model. I mentored a transgender student at the high school where I taught; he was struggling with his identity and faced family struggles similar to what I faced at his age. In the secondary school where I taught, several other students reached out and asked me about my story and where they could find support. There were many LGBTQ staff members in the school, but there wasn't a large out LGBTQ student community. It was almost like déjà vu witnessing young, passionate students struggling to embrace their identities and make change in their own communities at the same time. It was a life-changing experience to pass on my guidance, wisdom, and experience to future young leaders.

Another immensely satisfying part of my journey has been my mother's transition from a supportive parent to an outright LGBTQ advocate. She has always loved me for who I am, and for that I will be forever grateful. When I told her I identified as male, she began learning as much as she could about transgender people and the issues we face. Indeed, my mom is a role model for how to be a loving and supportive parent. As she gained understanding, she asked questions. She knew that she was not an expert and that she did not have all of the answers. But as long as I was willing to give her the time to grow, she was willing to rise to the occasion. We had many talks; not all of them were easy, but they were essential for both of us to find our way alongside my new identity. She is now a transgender activist. She has spoken to the General Assembly and lobbied Virginia senators and delegates in support of LGBTQ rights. I could not be more proud to be her son.

My mother, father, and siblings attended and supported my wedding to my wife, Poyani, which took place in London. It was the happiest day of my life, and the support of my mother was compounded that day by the beaming pride of my father. My mother was central to facilitating understanding between my father and me. This understanding and bond has changed my life for the better. Poyani and I both have the overwhelming love and support of our parents going forward, which gives us great happiness.

I have learned so much from every stage of my life, and I look forward to what the future holds. I am now pursuing a law degree at the University of Virginia in order to realize my dream of becoming a civil rights attorney. I want to help marginalized communities fight for their rights, and while I know from personal experience that it won't be easy, it is work that is central to who I am.

CONCLUSION

Jah Akande captures the heart of WILL* when he notes that students in the program "understand the intersections of race, gender, sexuality, and poverty, and the importance of translating that understanding into advocacy." That one quote distills the essence of the WILL* program. It reflects the importance of thinking in intersectional ways and then using that knowledge to take initiative and use one's voice and actions for the greater good. That ability to translate theoretical knowledge into practical application rests at the core of what makes WILL* a powerful student experience. Within this collection, each story, in its own unique way, reflects the bridging of theory and praxis. As Allison Speicher writes in the first story, "WILL* taught me that the things I saw and the way they made me feel could be a means of praxis, personal transformation, and social activism."

Ultimately, we would love to see the basic elements of the WILL* program that influenced these graduates widely embraced by many other universities, schools, and organizations. As the personal testimonies in this book make clear, the WILL* format works because it grounds idealism in knowledge about how power, privilege, and oppression work in all of our lives and our communities. It offers students the tools, skills, and structure necessary to take concrete action on issues of importance to them during and after their college years. It helps them understand that improving their communities takes intersectional analysis, intentional effort, and time. As the twelve stories in this book showcase, WILL* powerfully combines a feminist education and a commitment to understanding inequities with the audacity to address them.

The WILL* program model is flexible and transferable to many different kinds of schools and organizations. If you are interested in learning more about the mechanics of the WILL* program, or in replicating it, visit our website at http://will.richmond.edu.[1] There, you will find a "Program Replication" tab, which will take you to a "WILL* Replication Toolkit." This toolkit is a quick guide to starting your own program, and it contains valuable information for brainstorming how to do so at your school, institution, or in your community. For colleges and universities, you will find worksheets to help guide your planning and strategizing specifically at higher education institutions. These worksheets will help you assess your campus climate for this type of program and identify not only the strengths and challenges of starting a program but also how to nurture allies and anticipate barriers that may stand in your way. Another tool will walk you through identifying what you already have and what you still need to make the program work across a number of institutional constituencies, including students, staff, faculty, administrators, and governing boards. And of course, if you are thinking about creating a program, we hope you will reach out to us.

Your program need not look like ours. The adaptability of WILL* can be seen in the diverse programs that have been put in place at various colleges and universities. Each institution has created a program to suit its own unique context. For example, the Baldwin Scholars at Duke University is a replicated program, but their program includes two academic seminars rather than a minor, offers participants the opportunity to live together, and focuses heavily on leadership.

The WILL programs at the University of Cincinnati and the University of Michigan, Dearborn have been adapted for large public university settings in which most students commute and are older than traditionally aged college students.

We also look forward to hearing and learning about other programs beyond our own that blend feminist theory and praxis in substantial ways. We focus on WILL* here because it is the program we know best. It's been our paid, daily work for many years, and we continue to do the work because of how much meaning it holds for us and for the difference we see it make in students' lives day in and day out. For example, we have seen students of color who, for the first time, can name what they often experience as "microaggressions" and how those aggressions connect to white privilege. We have seen an intern confront a boss who expected her to take his clothes to the dry cleaner. We have seen a transgender student recognize and name transphobia while interning at one of the most well-known human rights organizations in the country. We have seen a student who grew up experiencing homelessness but had never spoken about it publically confront her feelings of shame as we addressed this topic in and outside of class. She came to embrace her past, speak about it freely, and use it to fuel her dedication to justice and equity. These incidents are not mere abstractions for us or for our students; they are real, everyday occurrences. Because of what they learn in the WILL* program, students have the consciousness and empathy to recognize inequality and the understanding and tools to address it.

WILL* cultivates and supports commitments to justice and equity, even when the problems of the world seem especially daunting. As Jennifer Stolarski concludes, "WILL helped me to identify my work. And by 'work,' I do not mean my career, though it is certainly intertwined in my work; I mean how I fit into the world and what I can give back. WILL taught me that I could effect change." It is this combination of analysis, activism, and hope that fuels participants' audacity.

As Courtney Martin writes in *The New Better Off*, the times that we live in may break our hearts, but they don't have to break our spirit.[2] We hope that this book captures that spirit, and that you carry it forward.

ENDNOTES

Introduction

1. This asterisk is more than just a footnote. When founded in 1980, the program was called Women Involved in Living and Learning, with the acronym of WILL. When the program explicitly opened to transgender and gender-nonconforming students in 2013, we dropped the name but kept the acronym, adding an asterisk to denote that the program now explicitly includes gender-expansive students as well as women.

2. WILL* alum Cammie Dunaway inspired the title of this book. Read her story to learn more about the "audacious" visions that informed her learning in the WILL* program.

3. *The New York Times*, "Women's Representation in U.S. Federal Government is Falling Behind Globally," August 21, 2016, http://nytlive.nytimes.com/womenintheworld/2016/08/21/womens-representation-in-u-s-federal-government-is-falling-behind-globally/

4. Ariane Hegewisch and Emma Williams-Baron, "The Gender Wage Gap 2016: Earning Differences by Race and Ethnicity," Institute for Women's Policy Research, https://iwpr.org/publications/gender-wage-gap-2016-weekly/

5. Shelley Correll, Stephen Benard, and In Paik, "Getting a Job: Is There a Motherhood Penalty," *American Journal of Sociology*, March 2007, Vol. 112, No. 5, 1297-1337.

6. Michelle Budig, "The Fatherhood Bonus and the Motherhood Penalty: Parenthood and the Gender Gap in Pay," *Third Way*, September 2, 2014, http://www.thirdway.org/report/the-fatherhood-bonus-and-the-motherhood-penalty-parenthood-and-the-gender-gap-in-pay

7. Workers may qualify for up to 12 weeks of unpaid, job-protected leave under the Family and Medical Leave Act (FMLA), passed in 1993. But the law only applies to certain employers and employees; scholars estimate that more than forty percent of all workers are not covered by FMLA. US Department of Labor, https://www.dol.gov/whd/fmla/chapter3.htm

8. Wendy Wang, Kim Parker, and Paul Taylor, "Breadwinner Moms," Pew Research Center, May 29, 2013, http://www.pewsocialtrends.org/2013/05/29/breadwinner-moms/

9. Bixby Center for Global Reproductive Health, University of California San Francisco, https://bixbycenter.ucsf.edu/sites/bixbycenter.ucsf.edu/files/Abortion%20restrictions%20risk%20women's%20health.pdf

10. Michael Lavers, "Report: 594 LGBT people murdered in Americas during 15-month period," *Washington Blade*, December 20, 2014, http://www.washingtonblade.com/2014/12/20/report-594-lgbt-people-murdered-americas-15-month-period/

11. Alicia Garza and L. A. Kauffman, "A Love Note to Our Folks: Alicia Garza on the Organizing of #BlackLivesMatter," *n+1* Magazine, January 20, 2015. "Queerness on the Front Lines of #BlackLivesMatter," MSNBC Digital Documentaries, February 19, 2015.

12. Dean Stephanie Bennett-Smith founded the WILL* program in conjunction with Dr. Jane Hopkins, Dr. Kathleen Rohaly, and Dr. William Walker.

13. Kimberlé Crenshaw, "Demarginalizing the Intersection of Race and Sex: A Black Feminist Critique of Antidiscrimination Doctrine, Feminist Theory, and Antiracist Politics," *University of Chicago Legal Forum*, 1989, 139–67.

14. For more information on intersectionality, see Kimberlé Crenshaw, "Mapping the Margins: Intersectionality, Identity Politics, and Violence against Women of Color," *Stanford Law Review* 43 (6): 1241-99 (1991).

15. Anna Julia Cooper, for example, articulated a Black feminist perspective in *A Voice from the South*, published in 1892. See Rudolph P. Byrd, Johnnetta Betsch Cole, Beverly Guy-Sheftall, eds., *I am Your Sister: Collected and Unpublished Writings of Audre Lorde* (Oxford: Oxford University Press, 2009), 8.

16. The Combahee River Collective Statement, 1977, http://circuitous.org/scraps/combahee.html

17. Cherríe Moraga and Gloria E. Anzaldúa, eds., *This Bridge Called My Back*: *Writings by Radical Women of Color* (Albany: State University of New York Press, 2015). Originally published in 1981.

18. For example, see Gloria T. Hull, Patricia Bell Scott, and Barbara Smith, eds., *All the Women Are White, All the Blacks Are Men, But Some of Us Are Brave: Black Women's Studies* (New York: The Feminist Press, 1982); bell hooks, *Ain't I A Woman: Black Women and Feminism* (Boston: South End Press, 1981); and Patricia Hill Collins, *Black Feminist Thought: Knowledge, Consciousness, and the Politics of Empowerment* (Boston: Unwin Hyman, 1990).

19. Paulo Freire, *Pedagogy of the Oppressed* (New York: Herder and Herder, 1972).

20. We want to be clear that this work is not about a "check your privilege" analysis, which is currently very prevalent on college campuses and often operates only at the level of the individual. Instead, it's about tackling systemic privilege and oppression and how those systems manifest in our daily lives.

21. bell hooks, *Teaching to Transgress: Education as the Practice of Freedom* (New York: Routledge, 1994), 15.

22. Marshall Ganz, "What is Public Narrative?," 2008, https://comm-org.wisc.edu/syllabi/ganz/WhatisPublicNarrative5.19.08.htm

23. Ibid.

24. At the time of this book's publication, WILL* is undergoing another name-change process. You will still be able to find information about the program through the University of Richmond's website, but know that when you look for it, the program will likely have a different name.

25. The first women's studies program in the United States started in 1970 at San Diego State College, now known as San Diego State University. Roberta Salper, "San Diego State 1970: The Initial Year of the Nation's First Women's Studies Program," *Feminist Studies* 37 (3): 658–682.

Chapter 1: Allison

1. William Alcott, *Confessions of a Schoolmaster,* (New York: Arno Press, 1969), 305. Originally published in 1839.

Chapter 9: Laura

1. An official average of twenty females die each year in "honor" crimes, although experts agree that actual numbers are likely higher because some deaths go unreported. Rothna Begum, "How to End 'Honor' Killings in Jordan," *The Jordan Times*, April 3, 2017. https://www.hrw.org/news/2017/04/03/how-end-honor-killings-jordan

2. Ragui Assad, Rana Hendy, and Chaimaa Yassine, "Gender and the Jordanian Labor Market," *Economic Research Forum*, 2012, http://archive.hhh.umn.edu/people/rassaad/pdf/Gender_in_Jordan.pdf

3. Official figures estimate that approximately 100,000 Jordanian women are married to non-Jordanians, most commonly Palestinians, Egyptians, Syrians, and Iraqis, leaving about 400,000 children without Jordanian citizenship.

Chapter 10: Jill

1. All names have been changed to protect privacy.

Chapter 12: Jah

1. My father and I are great friends now.

2. Since this time, the residential colleges at the University of Richmond, Westhampton College and Richmond College, have been working toward greater gender inclusion. For example, Westhampton explicitly welcomes students historically underrepresented by gender, including transgender and gender expansive students.

Conclusion

1. At the time of this book's publication, WILL* is under-going a name-change process. You will still be able to find information about the program through the University of Richmond's website, but know that when you look for it, the program will likely have a different name.

2. Courtney Martin, *The New Better Off: Reinventing the American Dream* (Boston: Da Capo Press), 2016.

ABOUT THE AUTHORS

Holly Blake is the director of the WILL* program and associate dean for outreach education and development at the University of Richmond. She has worked with WILL* since 1992 and is dedicated to helping students bridge feminist theory and praxis. She earned her PhD in history from Binghamton University and her research interests include the intersections of gender, race, class, and sexuality in the mid-nineteenth-century US, utopian socialism, and community-based learning pedagogy. She published "Marie Howland: 19th Century Leader for Women's Economic Independence" as a special edition of *The American Journal of Economics and Sociology* in November 2015.

Melissa Ooten is the associate director of the WILL* program and gender research specialist at the University of Richmond. She has worked with WILL* since 2005 and is deeply committed to educating the next generation of social justice advocates. She holds a PhD in history from The College of William and Mary and specializes in studying social movements in the US South. She published *Race, Gender, and Movie Censorship in Virginia, 1922–1965* with Rowman and Littlefield in 2015 and has written a number of articles on issues ranging from mass incarceration to eugenics to teaching #BlackLivesMatter through film.

Holly and Melissa have coauthored two previous pieces on the WILL* program: "Bridging the Divide: Connecting Feminist Histories and Activism in the Classroom," published in *Radical History Review* in fall 2008, and a short piece entitled "Connecting Theory and Practice," which appeared in the spring 2009 issue of *Ms. Magazine*.

Author photos © Kim Lee Schmidt and Gordon Schmidt

SELECTED TITLES FROM
SHE WRITES PRESS

She Writes Press is an independent publishing company founded to serve women writers everywhere. Visit us at www.shewritespress.com.

Times They Were A-Changing: Women Remember the '60s & '70s edited by Kate Farrell, Amber Lea Starfire, and Linda Joy Myers. $16.95, 978-1-938314-04-9. Forty-eight powerful stories and poems detailing the breakthrough moments experienced by women during the '60s and '70s.

Transforming Knowledge: Public Talks on Women's Studies, 1976-2011 by Jean Fox O'Barr. $19.95, 978-1-938314-48-3. A collection of essays addressing one woman's challenges faced and lessons learned on the path to reframing—and effecting—feminist change.

100 Under $100: One Hundred Tools for Empowering Global Women by Betsy Teutsch. $29.95, 978-1-63152-934-4. An inspiring, comprehensive look at the many tools being employed today to empower women in the developing world and help them raise themselves out of poverty.

Love Her, Love Her Not: The Hillary Paradox edited by Joanne Bamberger. $16.95, 978-1-63152-806-4. A collection of personal essays by noted women essayists and emerging women writers that explores the question of why Americans have a love/hate "relationship" with Hillary Clinton.

Green Shoots of Democracy in the Philadelphia Democratic Party by Karen Bojar. $16.95, 978-1-63152-141-6. Based on interviews with longtime and newly elected committee people and ward leaders speaking candidly about their experiences in the ward system, Green Shoots of Democracy within the Philadelphia Democratic Party is an in-depth analysis of partisan politics on the grassroots level.

Renewable: One Woman's Search for Simplicity, Faithfulness, and Hope by Eileen Flanagan. $16.95, 978-1-63152-968-9. At age forty-nine, Eileen Flanagan had an aching feeling that she wasn't living up to her youthful ideals or potential, so she started trying to change the world—and in doing so, she found the courage to change her life.